GW00392500

Gasligh

Turning the tables on the narcissist: master his favorite manipulation technique to be always one step ahead and be the only one in control

Dr. Stephanie Sharp

© Copyright 2019 - All rights reserved.

The content contained within this book may not be reproduced, duplicated or transmitted without direct written permission from the author or the publisher.

Under no circumstances will any blame or legal responsibility be held against the publisher, or author, for any damages, reparation, or monetary loss due to the information contained within this book. Either directly or indirectly.

Legal Notice:

This book is copyright protected. This book is only for personal use. You cannot amend, distribute, sell, use, quote or paraphrase any part, or the content within this book, without the consent of the author or publisher.

Disclaimer Notice:

Please note the information contained within this document is for educational and entertainment purposes only. All effort has been executed to present accurate, up to date, and reliable, complete information. No warranties of any kind are declared or implied. Readers acknowledge that the author is not engaging in the rendering of legal, financial, medical or professional advice. The content within this book has been derived from various sources. Please consult a licensed professional before attempting any techniques outlined in this book.

By reading this document, the reader agrees that under no circumstances is the author responsible for any losses, direct or indirect, which are incurred as a result of the use of information contained within this document, including, but not limited to, — errors, omissions, or inaccuracies.

Table of Contents

Introduction

Gaslighting occurs in personal relationships and professional relationships, and in other cases, gaslighting is used by public figures to change the perceptions of targeted members of the population.

Gaslighting is a form of psychological abuse. It can make you start to doubt your ability to perceive reality correctly. It can make you think you didn't see what you thought you saw or hear what you thought you heard; and you start to wonder if you can trust the information you are getting from your five senses. Moreover, this, in turn, will make you begin to think that there must be something wrong with you, and you will begin to doubt your sanity.

It doesn't matter whether it is happening in a personal relationship (parent to child, between romantic partners) or a professional relationship at work or even between members of the same community. Gaslighting creates an abusive situation which can cause serious health problems if the victim continues to be in such a position for a long time.

And no matter whether it occurs in a personal relationship or a working relationship, between a public figure and the members of the public or somewhere else, it is essential to be aware of the signs that you or someone you know might be a victim of gaslighting, as this awareness is the first step to getting out of the damaging situation.

The first step to take towards being free from gaslighting is to recognize exactly what gaslighting is. It is often very hard to recognize the signs of gaslighting, because they affect the mind so much that, after a long period of time, the victim doesn't trust their own thoughts.

This book discusses in detail how to distinguish gaslighting behavior from typical behavior by shedding light on the different kinds of gaslighting techniques. It also aims to provide you with information about what to do if you find yourself a victim of such a negative situation.

Gaslighting, which will be defined fully in the following chapters, is a technique used by narcissists to manipulate people. Narcissists are self-centered and arrogant people who lack empathy for others. They live in their own world and believe they are unique and special. Hence, they always seek attention and praise from others.

A narcissist will frequently use gaslighting, as a narcissist's goal is to disorient the victim to gain total control over them. A narcissist achieves this aim by gradually sowing seeds of doubt in the victim's mind, and in the end, the narcissist controls the victim to do their bidding.

In addition to promoting awareness about gaslighting, this book is written with the more precise aim of exposing the extent to which narcissists use gaslighting as a means of manipulation to control and abuse their victims both physically and mentally. They expose the words narcissists say and the actions they take to abuse victims. It is one thing to recognize what gaslighting is, and it is another to know how narcissists use it. It is also a different thing entirely to uncover the effects of gaslighting and guard against them - or better still, avoid the effects in the first place.

Most importantly, they show you how to protect yourself and even remove yourself from the control of a gaslighting narcissist.

Chapter 1. What is Gaslighting?

"Gaslighting" is a term coined from a play written by Patrick Hamilton in 1938 called *Gas Light;* and is one of the most insidious and damaging forms of manipulation. This tactic involves convincing another person that his or her perception of reality is damaged, inaccurate or entirely false altogether.

In the play, a man has discovered a secret area within his apartment building. When he enters the secret area and turns on the gas lights, the rest of the lights in his apartment dim somewhat, with the gas being redirected to the newly activated lights. His wife inevitably asks about the lights dimming when it happens, and he ultimately convinces her that the lights are *not* fading, and that it is only in her head.

This is gaslighting at its core. It seeks to create doubt in memory, sanity and perception of reality in a victim.

Gaslighting defies boundaries

When somebody is gaslighting   you, they are trying to convince you that your boundaries and perceptions are ridiculous and invalid.

If something they say bothers you because it is abusive or untrue, they will tell you that you are overreacting, or that what you are saying is stupid. They will tell you that it doesn't bother anybody else except you and that you're just being overly sensitive. Even spiritual people are not immune from this, because you might be told that their behavior wouldn't bother you if you were more enlightened. So, in essence, gaslighting and manipulation techniques make you doubt your boundaries or make you drop your boundaries altogether by convincing you that your boundaries are stupid and invalid.

The truth is that your boundaries aren't anybody's business but yours. Nobody gets to determine what boundaries you will have. If something bothers you, then nobody gets to tell you how you feel. Let's say that somebody's punching you in the arm over and over again, and you tell the person, "Please stop punching me in the arm," and the person says something like, "I'm not punching you that hard". It is not up to them to decide if the punching bothers you at all. It's up to you. When you enforce a boundary like that, you are not only fighting for the boundary itself, but, more importantly, for your right to set boundaries in the first place. Don't let another person convince you that your boundary isn't big enough for you to take a stand over. It is. Such a way of thinking is really disrespectful.

It's very disrespectful and dishonoring to stand on somebody else's boundary. There is a difference between controlling somebody else by telling them how to behave, and setting a boundary by which you are telling the person not to behave a certain way to you. Reinforcing a boundary means that you are going to have to walk away from someone or from something when they do something wrong to you. Now, realize that it's not about stopping someone from living their life the way they want to live their life, nor is it taking their freedom away from them. It's simply about choosing to engage with or not engage with people who behave in a certain way or who don't respect your boundaries.

Setting up an angry beast

The second form of manipulation is to become an angry beast. This is where somebody tries to become angrier than you when you get angry with them, in order to squash your challenge or rebellion. You might even be just mildly annoyed about something and want to talk to your partner about it, but they explode at you so that you find yourself backing down. You will be so shocked because you were talking about something which was relatively small, and they just turned it into something huge. You will want to back down and not deal with that type of drama. Often, you will be trying to defend your boundaries, and that is what causes the explosion.

4

This angry beast will come at you with an emotional response that is way out of proportion to the situation or the position that you're trying to defend. You will back down and, often times, you won't even try to stand up for yourself again because you are absolutely not willing to go up against that angry beast. The gaslighter is counting on that.

But when you are defending a proper boundary or setting a boundary, it doesn't really matter what the boundary is all about nor does it really matter whether that person sees it as valid or not. Once you have clearly communicated a boundary and the other person says that he will not accept it, you must follow through on the consequences or you will be intimidated into silence and submission. That is what the angry beast wants.

Hijacking the issue

The next manipulative technique is hijacking the issue. This happens when you raise a topic that challenges someone, and he takes it off on a tangent to distract you so that you will not set that boundary or defend that boundary. For example, let's say it's late at night and your spouse hasn't come home from work. They haven't called and you are really worried because you have no idea where they are or if something has happened to them. They finally come home, and you confront them with how worried you were, and ask them where they were and why they didn't even call you to let you know that they would be late.

Rather than answer your concern and questions, they go off on a tangent about how stressed they are at work and how you're not just getting it. They might start to get angry and accuse you of having no sympathy for them. You then find yourself on the defensive side of the conversation, and even apologize to them. Now you're no longer talking about the original topic – how late they were and why they didn't call – but talking about them, and what's bothering them. In the end, they will avoid answering your question altogether.

They have hijacked the conversation and turned it in a different direction. You will often find yourself sitting them down and apologizing to them, and feeling like you shouldn't bother them with your little concerns.

People who use these manipulation tactics are not doing so in a conscious way. They're not doing this on purpose. So they are not hijacking a conversation on purpose, but they are doing it none the less. They don't intend to work up to being an angry beast, or trample on your boundaries, but they do. They do it to control and manipulate you into always putting them first.

Chapter 2. What is A Narcissistic Personality?

The word 'narcissist' seems to be a buzzword that we hear a lot these days, but the truth is that genuine narcissists are actually rare. Nevertheless , many people are walking around with a whole host of narcissistic traits, making life very difficult for those around them.

Throughout this chapter, we're going to talk in great detail about narcissism. This is necessary to help you to be able to identify a narcissist if you bump into one, and also to help you examine whether the person you're in a relationship with, the person you may suspect of being a narcissist, truly is one or not.

Before we go on, we need to give a quick reality check. If you are in a relationship with a narcissist and you're struggling with the effects, you need to end this relationship and walk away. You will never be happy with a narcissist - it's impossible. They will always use their traits and tactics to control and belittle you, and you will never be on an even footing as a result. You will have a life of constantly doubting yourself and worrying - is that what you want?

Of course not!

To help you understand whether this is your situation or not, however, let's delve further into the world of the narcissist.

What is Narcissistic Personality Disorder?

Narcissistic Personality Disorder, or NPD, is a condition that fits under the personality disorder umbrella. It is not categorized as a mental health condition per se, but it does affect the way a person thinks, feels, reacts, and associates with those around them.

The main characteristic of narcissism is a lack of empathy. Narcissists cannot exhibit or feel empathy, and as a result, they cannot reciprocate emotions such as love, comfort, contentment, glee, excitement, or being happy for someone else. Instead, narcissists have an inflated sense of self-importance. They're very selfish, and they look at every situation in terms of what they can get out of it. They do not love in a normal way, simply because they are not able to compute the emotions related to love in the same way as everyone else.

Narcissism does not have a cure, but it can be managed via cognitive behavioral therapy methods and mindset training. This is a long and drawn-out process, and it requires complete commitment from the person in question. Of course, to access this treatment, the narcissist first needs to admit that they have a problem and need help. That in itself is the sticking point. Most narcissists never get help, simply because they do not believe there is anything wrong with them. They think the issue and fault lie with those around them instead. As a result, most narcissists are walking around undiagnosed and untreated. This increases the likelihood of you bumping into one, and being seduced into a relationship.

You might wonder how anyone could fall in love with a person so self-absorbed and lacking in empathy. At face value, that's a fair point. As with most manipulators, the person you meet at first will be nothing like the person behind the mask.

A narcissist is a wolf in sheep's clothing. They will be extremely charming, attentive and almost seem loving at first. They will wine and dine you, whisk you away, treat you like you mean the world to them, and charm the socks off you at the same time. You'll think you've met the most amazing man or woman, you might even think you've met The One.

This is an act, and it will continue tirelessly until you're completely attached. As soon as the narcissist is convinced that you're emotionally attached to them, they will very slowly peel off their mask, but only enough to allow them to put it back on again if you start to catch wind of their true self.

This change in behavior is not going to be instant. They will not go from loving and charming one minute, to cold and aloof the next. It will be a steady, slow drip of change, which is what makes it so confusing and dangerous. This will be enough to confuse you, to make you wonder whether you're imagining this change. As soon as the narcissist starts to think that maybe you're starting to have doubts, they will smoothly slip back into their former role, charming you back to where you were. This will be an ongoing pattern until you're so deeply invested emotionally, you can't see the forest for the trees.

An interesting paradox about narcissists is that, even though they have such an inflated sense of self-importance, they actually have a very low level of self-esteem. How can that be? Because their lack of confidence relates to their lack of emotions. They grab hold of people and hold them close because they're terrified that people are going to leave. They don't want you to have a life of your own or your own hobbies, because they become scared those friends or hobbies are going to draw you away from them. Maybe these things will help you to see through their mask and be the catalyst to your walking away. That is how a narcissist thinks.

Of course, in a normal and healthy relationship, both partners have their own space and time to do their own thing, to have something to talk about when they come back together again. This ensures the relationship flourishes and builds trust in one another. This is not something a narcissist will allow to happen. Instead, they will exert control in the most subtle of ways, to the point where you almost can't see it happening.

The Main Traits of a Narcissist

The main indicator of NPD is a lack of empathy. This isn't through choice however; this is an inability to recognize empathy as a vital part of human life. A narcissist will not be able to recognize emotions in other people. For instance, if their partner is feeling worried and down, they probably won't see it and will instead focus on their own lives and their own needs, constantly putting demands on their partner and probably worsening the problems as a result.

9

Aside from a lack of empathy, the main traits of a narcissist and things to recognize are:

- An inflated sense of self-importance,

- A desire to have the best things in life, e.g. they have to have the best cell phone, the fanciest car, the promotion at work that everyone else wants,

- They usually try and associate themselves with people of high social standing or in management positions,

- They are never wrong about anything, everyone else is wrong instead,

- They value their own opinion over everyone else's; their opinion is gospel and everyone else's views are ridiculous,

- They will turn everything around on you and make it your fault, even if they are genuinely to blame,

- They will use gaslighting as a common tactic, i.e. making you question your own sanity,

- A total lack of self-confidence underneath it all,

- A constant need for praise,

- The ability to exploit other people without feeling shame or guilt about it,

- They often live in a fantasy world which is in line with their inflated sense of self,

- They expect everyone to do as they ask, to act on their whims,

- Exert control over others,

- Use alienation tactics, to pull people away from their support system,

- Usually, have a long history of failed relationships,

- Find it very difficult to maintain friendships,

• They are extremely charming and seem loving at first, but it's an act to draw you in. They can also switch this act on and off whenever they need to.

Narcissists don't always show every single one of the traits mentioned on that list, and they may have a few, most of them, or even some different traits. Every single person on the planet is individual, whether narcissistic or not. Because of this, you should look out for the traits listed, but be open-minded in terms of their severity.

However, none of the traits mentioned is particularly positive. A narcissist will turn every single thing against you and cause you to believe it's your fault. They will twist and turn everything around until you're not sure which way is upside down, left or right, and you will find yourself in a constant push and pull war - you love them but you don't like them at the same time.

When you start to think you should leave, they spot this and turn on the charm, causing you to remember why you fell for them in the first place. As a result, most people stick around, and the vicious circle begins once more.

Chapter 3. Types of Narcissistic Abuse

It is important to emphasize that narcissistic abuse is not only about cruelty and violence. If narcissistic abuse were that obvious, there would be more answers and fewer victims today. Narcissistic abuse comes in many forms. It can occur in subtle ways and you need to know what to look for before you can recognize a narcissist.

This chapter will shed light on the various weapons in the arsenal that narcissists use to manipulate. It will now dawn on you why you have been second-guessing yourself and having trouble believing in yourself even when the issue was right in front of you.

Outburst: Narcissist Reaction to Shame

Have you been alarmed by a narcissist's violent reaction to even the smallest bit of offense? We need to understand their personality to be able to answer this. Narcissists react to a threat to their ego with a narcissist outburst. The rage can be in two forms: passive-aggressive or explosive.

With the passive-aggressive outburst, the narcissist withdraws into the silent treatment for long periods to punish their partner.

The explosive outburst is characterized by highly volatile expression of displeasure.

Even though their outbursts and rage might be similar, there is a big difference between them. What triggers an extreme narcissist outburst can be so minute that it would trigger only mild anger or annoyance in others. Disagreeing with a sane person might result in anger. However, with a narcissist, it will trigger rage, because a disagreement to them is challenging their idealized version of the world, which does not sit well with them.

You might be turned off after experiencing a narcissist's rage stages in the early days of your relationship. You will probably relive the sequence of events over and over to try and wrap your head around what could have warranted such an attack. What you do not understand is that you are not to blame for triggering the narcissist outburst. The rage is the narcissist's default response to shame.

Causes of a Narcissist's Rage

Trying to wrap your head around the events that triggered a narcissist rage is futile. The root cause can be traced back to their faulty personality disorder. A susceptible temperament, along with a void during the early development stages, is what can cause a narcissistic personality disorder. Emotional outbursts are inherent in all humans, by nature. Children resort to these primitive outbursts as a means of expressing unmet needs.

Anger is a result of various stages of emotions. The interesting thing is that there is a certain amount of control you can exert on each stage. These levels exist from mild to extreme, and expression differs from one person to another. A psychologist, Adam Blatner classified the levels of anger into seven. (Blatner, 2005)

1. Stress: A subconscious feeling of anger without any visible reaction

2. Anxiety: Anger coming out through small clues

3. Agitation: Signs of displeasure without aggression

4. Irritation: An increased sign of displeasure

5. Frustration: Anger with harsh words

6. Anger: Raised voice and mild aggression

7. Outburst/Rage: Wrath with uncontrollable aggression

This is the progression of anger in normal people. The narcissist, however, automatically transcends to the seventh stage. All it takes to trigger the narcissist's outburst is a little scratch of their ego. They are filled with exaggerated idealized opinions which are responsible for the outburst. Any threat to their ego is met with a violent outburst as a means to keep their self-image intact.

Therefore, a narcissist outburst is a primitive method of protecting and defending themselves against any shame. A careful study of a narcissist will reveal that their rage is always characterized by jealousy, hatred, verbal abuse, demeaning others, etc. They, however, can control this behavior most of the time. It is when the narcissist's defense is down or affected by circumstances beyond their control that they resort to the narcissist outburst.

Unlike anger, narcissists' outburst is not a reaction to stress. It is a result of fear of not having their needs met. A narcissist, being a hypersensitive individual, will always be on the lookout for threats, humiliations, or criticism. They consider this as a humiliating rejection, a deliberate action to provoke, which triggers an outburst, and they direct a cold and aggressive response in a bid to devalue the person who has threatened them. Most of the time, a narcissist's rage is not merited, which hinders judgment. That is why they resort to shouting, groundless accusations, and other manipulation techniques in a bid to get the person to back down.

Since narcissists are not developed emotionally, they are hypersensitive. This enables them to give a personalized and intense reaction to whatever happens. Being out of touch with their real self, they are usually entangled with the person who is unfortunate enough to be the source of their narcissistic needs.

This entanglement makes the other person responsible for soothing and inflating their ego, safety, purpose, sense of value, etc. In other words, this person is held accountable for the narcissistic person's wholeness, not their own. Most of the time, this person might believe he is in a normal two-way relationship, ignorant of the impact of the narcissist in his life.

Gaslighting: How the Narcissist Distorts Their and Your Reality

You were once confident in yourself and your abilities. You knew what you wanted and to some degree how to get it. Now, you realize how suspicious and catty you are towards others, and you are constantly in a state of doubt. You are not even sure of what you want or who you are. That high level of confidence that kept you afloat has somehow vanished.

You might even think there is something wrong with you, and you need help. But chances are, you are just fine. If any of the above sounds familiar, you could be a victim of gaslighting manipulation.

It is one of the favorite tools of narcissistic personalities and could be deliberate or unintentional. One of the aims of gaslighting is to gain power and control over the other person by making him question his sense of reality. Gaslighting is common in families, politics and work environments as well as romantic relationships.

"You never remember things correctly, I'm not surprised that you're so sure of something that never happened!" – The Gaslighter will constantly deny things that clearly happened so the other person will start questioning his own memories. If you can't trust your own memories, you will have to trust your gaslighter's, who will distort the reality for his own convenience.

"You always make such a drama of everything! You always have to ruin everything!" – In a relationship with a gaslighter, guilt and blaming are constant. Isn't attacking the best defense tool?

"This is not how it works. You're so stupid. Luckily you have me. I don't know how you would survive without me" – Creating codependency is the main goal of this kind of manipulation. Leading the victim to feel dependent, needy and incapable of making the most basic decisions is the way to have a perfect prey to control and decide for.

How to Know You Are Being Gaslighted

If any of these next points describes you, there is a big chance you might be a victim of gaslighting:

You get anxious more often and have a low level of confidence.

You feel you can't seem to do anything right.

You feel things go wrong because of you.

You apologize a lot.

You sense something is not right, but you cannot pinpoint what it is.

You wonder if you give the appropriate response to your partner.

You have no confidence when making hard decisions.

You have an underlying feeling of hopelessness and little to no pleasure in activities you once loved.

Forms of Gaslighting

Gaslighting is not an obvious form of manipulation. You must know what to look for before you know your partner is trying to distort your sense of reality. Some forms of gaslighting are:

Obvious Lying

People who gaslight never admit the truth even if you know they are lying. It is disturbing, how someone could lie and distort fact without an iota of remorse. It forms an abusive pattern which makes the victim become unsure of even the simplest thing. This resulting self-doubt is the aim of the abuser.

Using What You Love Against You.

Bear in mind that part of the overall aim of the gaslighter is to get you to question yourself. They want you to lose faith in yourself so that you question your dreams and life choices. This is why another form of manipulation is to use what is closest to their victim against them. If you love going to the cinema, they will find issues with it. If you have close friends, they will find a thousand and one reasons why they are not good friends. The aim is to make you question yourself and what you hold most dear.

Confusion

The fact that people love stability is obvious to the gaslighter. However, with the constant cycle of confusion and abuse, the victim *craves* clarity and stability. Unfortunately, the victim often turns to the gaslighter for it, which continues and reinforces the cycle of abuse.

Denying facts

They might make you a promise but deny ever making it. The gaslighter, in a bid to appear credible, will even ask you for proof of their statements. However, all you have is your memory and nothing concrete to show for it. This can make you start losing faith in your ability to recall the truth or let emotions cloud judgment. You might start accepting the fact that the person is right, and they never promised what you thought.

Everyone is a Liar

The gaslighter could tell you that everyone is lying to you. This is a tactic that forces you to lose faith in your sense of reality even more, and turn to them for everything. This keeps the cycle of the abuse intact.

Further Examples

A narcissist who gaslights is skilled at getting on their victim's nerves. Their interactions with you have revealed any weakness and vulnerability, making it easy to use this knowledge against you. With time, you doubt your memory and judgment, doubt yourself, and even question your sanity.

They tell you everyone is talking about you behind your back. They tell you your friends and loved ones think you are becoming unstable.

They deny things they previously said. "I didn't tell you I was going to take Jack to school. Now he's going to be scolded for being late."

Hiding things from you and deny knowing it. "You seriously can't find the keys? You just had them."

Whatever attempt you make to understand and clarify things will be met with anger.

Be careful of the toxic ones, especially if you are in a relationship with one. The fact that they are in a relationship with you makes it easy for them to play these mind games on you. On the surface, they might seem harmless, making it confusing. For instance, they might say: "I could never do that, you mean so much to me."

They will find a way to make it seem like your concern is baseless. This way, they turn the issue around and make it about you. For example, if you confront them about coming home late every night, they tell you they are working or just hanging out and that you obviously have trust issues.

Even though many of the things these people say may seem normal and likely harmless, the narcissist's aim is to distort the victim's sense of reality. As a result, the victim turns to the abuser to validate their feelings which then becomes the norm in the relationship.

Boundary Violation: The Narcissist Neither Understands nor Respects Them

Boundaries are essential in life, even though many people have no regard for personal space. We have markers and fences in our front yard that serve as boundaries. We have a gate in front of our house to keep away unwanted people and the elements. People respect physical limitations since they are clear signs to keep others in check.

Personal boundaries, on the other hand, are not visible. This makes it easy for other people to violate them, especially a narcissist. People who have been in a relationship with a narcissist know that one of the hallmarks of healing and recovery is having and enforcing healthy boundaries.

One of the twisted beliefs that exists in the mind of a narcissist is that others exist to serve them, especially their victim. As a result, they believe their need is way more important than the needs of others. They have no real sense of being, so they rely on others for power. They have an excessive need for attention and will milk their victims to the point of exhaustion.

Because of this, a major characteristic of people with narcissistic personality disorder is a complete disregard for boundaries. This affects their relationships with people at work as well as at home. Even in social settings, they are often viewed as inappropriate because they are the ones that dominate the conversation or make an insensitive remark.

Personal boundaries can be physical, mental, or emotional limits. They are there to guard us from manipulation and unfair treatment. The boundaries are there to put a distinction between your wants and feelings and those of others. This, most times, does not sit well with the narcissist, because they see it as rejection. They take it as cruelty on their feelings, emotions, and needs. A narcissist can be likened to a toddler that throws tantrums at every objection to their needs. It is a childish and immature way to relate to people.

This explains why a boundary does not work with a narcissist. Confident folks with good self-esteem will not put up with the mind games and tactics of a narcissist for long. A narcissist interprets this as not caring about them.

Everything a narcissist wants and does is based on emotions and fulfillment (How it makes them feel and what is in it for them.) This is why a strong boundary is a rejection because it cuts off all avenues of getting what they want. Their power play is unavailable, so they can't use this person's emotion to feel better.

Even though narcissists and empaths attract each other like magnets, narcissists are drawn to other people as well. They are drawn to whoever can be a source of their supply. This is why people with high social class, influence, and money also interest the narcissist. The difference, however, is that people who have firm boundaries and a clear standing on what they want do not indulge the narcissist. Setting boundaries involves being in tune with what you want and honoring that.

Violating boundaries comes in different forms, for example:

● People violate physical boundaries when they come into your personal space and make you uncomfortable. It also happens when people touch you, grab your things, or go through your phone, camera, or laptop without permission.

● Your emotional boundary can be violated by someone belittling or invalidating your feelings.

● A person violates your time boundary when he demands an excess amount of your time. This is common in narcissist relationships, since the abuser limits your time with friends and loved ones.

● Violation of a material boundary happens when someone takes your things or money without permission, or willfully damages your things.

Having a boundary involves knowing when to draw the line with other people; the narcissist especially. With whatever boundary you have in place, expect the narcissist to push it. The way narcissists are wired, there is no discrepancy between their feelings and those of others. They will accuse you of making them feel bad somehow. They will abuse and project their feelings on you. With a strong boundary, however, you will not think twice about dismissing them and calling the relationship off.

This is why boundaries do not augur well with a narcissist. Since they will push it, you have got to be firm with it. It is one of the strongest weapons to protect yourself and keep your sanity intact. The word "boundary" does not exist in the dictionary of the narcissist. They neither understand nor respect them. It is what they do. Setting boundaries and expecting compliance is like a whole different world to them. It disturbs their equilibrium, and will be met with strict displeasure and strong outburst.

Reciprocation: The Narcissist Does Not Reciprocate

If you have been through hell while in a relationship with a narcissist, one of the reasons is the absence of reciprocation. Many people have invested their spirit, soul, and body into a relationship with a narcissist without getting anything substantial in return. This is not surprising, because a narcissist lives in an idealized world in which he's supposed to be loved, worship and catered to.

As a result, no matter how much you sacrifice for a narcissist, they will not reciprocate. They do not know what love means neither do they love themselves; hence, they cannot love you back. This is why a relationship with a narcissist is draining. You do all the work, and it seems like you are the only one working for the relationship. No matter how sincere and dedicated you are to the relationship, it does not make a difference.

That adage: "If you don't love yourself, you can't love anybody else," explains the narcissist's lack of reciprocity. Their habits and behavior are rooted in a deep hatred of themselves. Even though they trick you into dating them, it is still hard for them to process the concept of loving someone other than themselves, let alone accepting that someone loves them too. This is why anything you do in the relationship to make a change is a futile effort that will not get you anything in return.

This is what makes a relationship with a narcissist abnormal. Not only is the relationship devoid of affection, but it is also like walking into a war zone. This is because you are handing your life over to someone who doesn't care about destroying it. They are dangerously jealous and care about themselves alone. They are only after what they can get from you and what makes them feel better.

If a narcissist gets close to you, it is because they see you as a source of what is called 'narcissistic supply'. To them, you are not human; therefore, they won't treat you like one. You only exist as a tool and means to soothe their ego, to take out their frustration on, build them up and meet their needs. That is their supply. This is just how narcissists are wired. With this in mind, do not get the wrong impression if you are in a relationship with a narcissist. They only need you to make themselves feel good. You exist to validate them. For instance, they believe that as long as someone loves them, they are important. This is all that matters, not that they want to share their goals, aspirations or life with another person.

Without a doubt, you exist and you are worthy. You are an individual with important goals and needs just like the rest of us. Unfortunately, as long as these things do not involve the narcissist, it doesn't interest him. To break free, it's important to understand that relationships with narcissistic personalities are not the symbiotic type. They're strictly about them, and there is no place for support, understanding and reciprocity.

Narcissists are only focused on themselves and what makes them tick. There is no room for any other person, no matter how you bend over backwards to make life easier for them and attend to their needs. They will not do anything for you in return.

Invalidation: A Narcissist's Weapon to Erase You

Many people in a relationship with a narcissist often get the feeling that they are invisible. Like they do not matter, and their opinions are worthless. This is not surprising; it is just another weapon in the arsenal of a narcissist. It is the basis for all forms of abuse and has devastating and damaging effects.

Remember that one of the key attributes of a narcissist is a lack of empathy. This explains why invalidation is a comfortable spectrum for a narcissist to operate within. Invalidation involves intentionally rejecting, minimizing, ignoring, or shunning your actions, concerns, emotions, and thoughts. It can be aggressive and overt, similar to bullying tactics. It can also be gentle and subtle like gaslighting.

Invalidation is one of the many snares they use to entangle victims. It boils down to the fact that narcissists have a distorted thinking pattern that fuels the invalidation: the thinking that only their needs, emotions and concerns have any value. An understanding of this will help victims fight and de-personalize this attack. The ability to understand this will help you realize that their invalidation is not about you; rather, it is about them.

When narcissists invalidate you, what they are doing, in reality, is telling you that your feelings and thoughts are irrelevant. In other words, your opinions, and feelings do not matter and you have no right to express them out loud. One sad thing about this form of abuse is that it destroys you gradually without your even realizing it. You may sense that something is wrong, but you cannot really pinpoint it because the narcissist doesn't want you to know the exact reason.

It is so insidious because if you consider the statement on the surface, it looks innocent. For instance, they use harsh statements like "You are blowing this out of proportion" or "Will you grow up." This is indirectly telling you that your feelings are irrelevant. The chronic ones will not only dismiss your feelings, but they will also tell you what they think your feelings are. Some will go as far as even ignoring your feelings. The next section discusses various ways a narcissist might invalidate you.

Examples of Invalidation

Mandating you to feel differently. For example, saying things like:

Cheer up.

Don't cry.

Don't worry.

Stop whining.

Deal with it.

Give it a rest.

Don't be so dramatic.

Grow up.

Get over it.

Stop feeling sorry for yourself.

Telling you to how to look. Saying things like:

Don't look so proud of yourself.

Don't look so dejected.

Don't look so serious.

Don't make that face.

Undermining your perception. Saying things like:

You are wrong.

I was just kidding.

It is not what it looks like.

You are getting it all wrong.

That is not right.

This is absurd.

That won't happen.

Trying to make you feel guilty. Saying things like:

I tried to warn you.

You are making me uncomfortable.

Trivializing your feelings. Saying things like:

It is not that bad.

You are being dramatic.

It is not enough to get you upset.

Nothing is wrong with you.

You are being completely irrational.

Judging you. Saying things like:

You have a problem.

You are too sensitive.

You are too emotional.

You are over-reacting.

You are impossible.

Trying to make you question yourself. Saying things like:

What is the matter with you?

Why can't you let this go?

Why must you always…?

It's just a joke. Why don't you get it?

Why must you always feel sorry for yourself?

Dictating your feelings and actions. Saying things like:

You should be happy that...

You better drop it.

This should not bother you so much.

You should just forget it.

You should be ashamed of yourself.

Using Dismissive Clichés. Saying things like:

In time you will understand.

Look at the bright side.

This is just a phase.

Everything has its reasons.

Time heals all wounds.

Narcissists and Lack of Attachment

It is not in the DNA of narcissists to attach emotionally to another person. True emotional connection does not exist in their makeup. Again, this has nothing to do with you.

Even during the onset of the relationship, you might think they validated you. This is both right and wrong. What you had then can be called "love-bombing" which involved them meeting your emotional needs. Remember, they were trying to get you entangled in their web. They will try everything in their capacity to do this even if it means being someone they are not. They needed you to love them and get attached. This was why they showered you with love, and it seemed like they cared. You thought you were loved, appreciated, valued, and understood. Whereas in reality, they mirrored your likes and dislikes, all in a bid to get you entangled.

Once they have you in their web, they show their true colors. It is not in the nature of a narcissist to love because that would mean being vulnerable and letting their guard down. Their need to feel superior makes them incapable of that.

To understand invalidation, it is important that we explore the flip side — validation.

Defining Validation

Humans are wired with basic needs. We all crave to be relevant and to belong. These are social needs that are as essential as other survival needs like food, shelter, and clothing. We want to feel connected to others and be validated, as it is a core part of having our needs met.

Validation involves supporting, recognizing, and acknowledging someone's thoughts, emotions and feelings without any attempt to alter them. It involves acceptance from others while also accepting ourselves. It is about being seen, heard, understood and valued. It goes hand in hand with empathy since it involves appreciating and acknowledging the emotional state of other people.

It is the hallmark of a true and healthy relationship. A relationship in which two people truly care about each other and seek to share each other's joy and sadness. Not only will your partner say they care, but their actions will show it.

Chapter 4. How To Recognize A Gaslighter

Narcissists use gaslighting to gain control over their victims, and when the victims cannot prove that the narcissist said something or acted in a particular way, they often go back to the narcissist for what reality is, or they hold the narcissist's version of events as real.

So, what are the cues narcissists pick up on to drive their victims crazy? How does a narcissist operate to make their victims insane? To understand how narcissists use gaslighting to make victims think they are deranged, it is necessary to look into a few things narcissists do and say before we paint a bigger picture of how they operate.

The narcissist will twist words to create images in the mind of the victim. In a bid to make the victim question what their reality is all about, the narcissist will say things about the victim's life, friends, family and possessions, among other topics.

Saying negative things about a victim's primary relationships is one of the ways a narcissist will seek to manipulate the victim. This is the very first maneuver a narcissist will use to make victims think that they are crazy.

Not only will narcissists make their victims doubt their mother, father, siblings, or best friends, narcissists will go further and make their victims question the intentions of the people that care so much about them. This happens because the narcissist wants to isolate their victim so that they can gain total control over their life. They also perceive people who love the victim as obstacles to their plans.

Why would a narcissist seek to do this evil thing? Well, narcissists are aware that the victim's loved ones will always support them and will bring them back to a state of sanity; so not only will narcissists question the intentions of the victim's loved ones, narcissists will drop subtle accusations about a victim's loved ones so as to create a breach of trust.

Another way a narcissist will make the victim think they are crazy is by projecting their negative actions onto the victim. A narcissist is never at fault for anything, so they make it the victim's fault when they are confronted for any wrongdoing. Even when a narcissist makes a mistake, instead of admitting it was their mistake, they will blame the victim. The victim is always responsible.

Let's take a break here to consider the story of a well-raised child who left home for college and made all the wrong choices while there, dropped out and then returned home to put all the blame on his parents. This is an example of a narcissistic child who is refusing to take responsibility for his actions. Instead, he is blaming the parents who have done their all to raise a good child.

Many times, when narcissists are caught doing exactly what they said they would not do by their victims, they magically turn the tables and all of a sudden, the victims are responsible for their wrongdoing.

Narcissists do not only project their wrong actions on others, but they project lies too, and when they are confronted with lying, they can turn it around to make it seem that it was the victim who was lying or it was the victim who made them lie.

Besides undermining their victim's relationships and putting the blame for their misdeeds on the victims, another way narcissists seek to make their victim think they are crazy is through mismatching words and deeds. They say a thing and go on to do another thing.

It is easy for a gaslighting narcissist to say one thing and do another. This is because a narcissist is a great salesperson who can get people to invest in them emotionally. A narcissist is the kind of person who will continually tell a victim, "I love you" but will never go out of their way to be there or show that they genuinely feel love.

Narcissists will make promises and never back them up. When the victims are too emotionally invested in them, they think that maybe one day the narcissist will follow through on their promise. This waiting for the follow-through that will never come can put the victim into a psychological mess as their sense of identity and self-esteem are attached to a lie.

However, it is essential to note that there are times when narcissists intentionally show acts of kindness, and this is another way in which they seek to manipulate the victim to think they are crazy. They keep victims confused when, in the midst of all their gaslighting acts, they do something for the victim that seems to be selfless.

These random acts of kindness are just hooks to draw the victim deeper and deeper into confusion, and they do this when they realize the victim is about to pull away from the deception. After they have used gaslighting on their victims for a while, they do something extraordinary and declare that they are well-intentioned.

At this point, it is worth noting that there are times when victims present cues that make it easy for the narcissist to continue to manipulate and control their reality. So, what are the signals narcissists pick up on to manipulate their victims into thinking they are crazy?

1.   The victim displays an emotional or relational vulnerability

Psychological vulnerabilities like past hurts, needs, or emotions can expose a victim to gaslighting from a narcissist. They might give out too much information that can make the narcissist step all over them by revealing intimate emotions or experiences. While trying to make the victim sound crazy, a narcissist might say something like "How did you come to a conclusion like that?" The narcissist will do this intentionally so that the victim starts to second-guess themselves.

2.   The victim reveals a personal issue of concern

Similar to displaying an emotional vulnerability, revealing wishes, desires and a bit of the inner person can leave a victim open to a gaslighting narcissist who could use this information as an opportunity to give wrong advice or interpretations to confuse the victim.

3.   The victim makes an error or a miscalculation

This happens in professional relationships in most cases. Making mistakes is a normal part of life, but narcissists can exploit others' mistakes to manipulate them. They are hyper-vigilant and too often possess good memories to keep track of another person's life. So, when a narcissist knows you made a little mistake, they jump in with words that will bring you down.

4.   The victim tries to create harmony

This is when a victim approaches a narcissist with the mindset of creating a win-win situation for both the narcissist and the victim. Unknown to most victims, narcissists will only seek to win for themselves and might use such cases to an unfair advantage. This peacemaking attempt can also happen in a situation where the victim realizes their mistake and tries to seek the forgiveness of a narcissist.

5.   The victim is trying to be helpful

The gaslighting narcissists will still find fault with a kind person. They do not have empathy and will always look for an angle to pounce on their victim.

Narcissists will look for any of these cues to disorient their victim and make them think they are crazy.

Here are specific tactics narcissists use to confuse their victims:

·   Baiting

Baiting means luring the victim with a false sense of security. By pretending to be good listeners (which they never are), a narcissist learns about the victim's flaws and insecurities and will use this knowledge later on to provoke the victim.

Baiting also means provoking the victim, and when the victim shows his disappointment, the narcissist will insist that he did not mean to make him angry or to hurt his feelings. He will look compassionate, loving and caring, reminding the victim of why he trusted him and liked him in the first place.

·   Love Bombing

Gaslighting narcissists will often use love bombing in the early phases of a relationship. Love bombing involves a narcissist overwhelming the victim with attention, flattery, compliments, or romance.

Being showered with attention looks good on the surface, but what the victim does not know is that these gestures are made to manipulate them further.

Love bombs are aimed at gaining your affection and trust. When a narcissist knows they have your faith, they are in charge and will start to control you to get what they need. At the end of the day, they want the relationship to just profit them, and after some time, you will be tossed aside to try to recover from your emotional injuries.

So here lies another problem. It is extremely hard to see love bombing when it is happening; but here are signs to look for:

1. Everything is happening way too fast

A narcissist will fall in love with you or display signs of affection to you more quickly than you have ever experienced before. They will make you feel that you're flawless. They may even reveal to you that you're the love of their lives they have been waiting for. Not too long after they meet you, they are showering you with gifts.

That doesn't mean you can't trust a new relationship, but you ought to be careful of any relationship that seems to appear unexpectedly out of nowhere. When it comes to falling in love with someone, the narcissist makes the magic seem real, but the reality is much different.

Know for a fact that true love grows slowly and recognize when things are moving too fast.

2. You are always being asked about the things that don't seem to be working in your life.

When someone you just met is always curious to know the things you have difficulties with or the things that don't seem to be working in your life, be careful of such a person. A narcissist will continuously ask you such questions because they want to provide solutions for you so that you think they are the savior that has finally come to rescue you.

What you might not notice is that they are asking about these things so that you think they are so awesome and caring, not because they genuinely care. They are also storing more information about you to be used against you later on in the relationship.

3.   They disrespect other people.

Narcissists can disrespect everyone, but they particularly disrespect people they perceive as of a lower status than themselves. Did you know that it's statistically proven that narcissists tend to disrespect waiters?

If you observe this in a relationship and you notice that it is a pattern that repeats itself, then consider it as a warning sign.

4. Nothing feels steady in the relationship

Later on, in your new relationship, you might start to experience a never-ending cycle of emotions. One moment you feel great, then the next moment you start feeling like a terrible human being. Healthy relationships don't go this way, most parts of healthy relationships are stable.

That's what a narcissist does, and they are quite skilled at it: when they compliment you, you feel like the best person in the world and then later, when they put you down and abuse you, you feel like the worst person in the world.

- Covert threats

"Do this or I will do that."

Covert threats happen when a victim challenges a notion or demand of a narcissist. The narcissist has a false sense of superiority and will see themselves as superiors who should not be challenged, so when the victim does not live up to their expectation or challenges them in any way, they feel threatened and will attempt to instill fear.

If somebody's response to your having a differing opinion from their own is to threaten you into submission, regardless of whether it is a subtle threat or an unmistakable declaration of what they intend to do, this is a warning sign that the person has a false sense of superiority.

Rather than solve disagreements maturely, narcissists will attempt to instill fear in you about what will happen if you do not choose to comply with them.

When someone threatens you in any way, pay attention and let them know you mean business by standing up for yourself, record their threats, and report them when possible.

- Name-calling

Name-calling is another tactic of gaslighting narcissists. It is an easy way to put victims down, so a gaslighting narcissist won't hesitate to call the behavior of the victim "stupid" or "dumb" just to insult the victim's intelligence and degrade them.

Name-calling is one of the last techniques gaslighting narcissists resort to when they can't think of a better way to invalidate your opinion. It is the easiest way to put you down. Name-calling is also used to demean your intelligence and appearance.

Rather than actually address a current topic at issue, a narcissist will attack you as a person because they feel threatened and only they are right. When a narcissist calls you all sorts of negative things, it is best not to internalize them and realize that they are seeking to undermine you because of their grandiose sense of self-importance.

· Shaming

"You should be ashamed of yourself…"

This is one of the favorite sayings of a gaslighting narcissist. When a narcissist feels challenged in any way, they use shaming to hit at their victim's self-esteem. They can do this because they know about some abuse or injustice a victim has suffered in the past. They enjoy opening past wounds to re-traumatize victims to make them feel unworthy.

Shaming is essentially an attempt at making you feel less than yourself by the narcissist.

If you suspect you are in a relationship with a narcissist, do not reveal any of your vulnerabilities or past injuries. Don't show anything from your past to people who have not convinced you of their good characters.

· Condescending Jokes

Gaslighting narcissists enjoy making malicious jokes at the expense of the victim, and they get away with saying abusive things in the form of jokes and will often accuse the victim of having no sense of humor when they are confronted.

Narcissists will use these kinds of derogatory jokes in gaslighting the victim, and in the end, the victim knows they have been abused by the narcissist but will still think it was just a joke after all.

Narcissists will also use sarcasm to tear the victim down, and if the victim reacts, they will label them as "sensitive." This will drive the victim into always double-checking their thoughts before they express them in words and they will begin to silence themselves.

· Control

Gaslighting narcissists are control freaks who want to control anything they can in the victim's life. They want to manage every facet of the victim's life; their finances, their friends, their time, their hobbies, and so on.

They want control because the more power they have over the victim, the more the victim will rely on them.

· Triangulation

"Even (name) thinks you are crazy."

Triangulation is bringing the opinion or perspective of a third party into a relationship. In romantic relationships, triangulation can also mean bringing in another person to form a love triangle so that the victim will feel insecure. Narcissists use other people's opinions to validate their own perspectives.

Narcissists often triangulate their partners in romantic relationships with strangers, colleagues, friends, and relatives to evoke jealousy. This is a diversionary strategy intended to pull the victim's focus away from identifying the abusive situation and paint a false image of themselves as a desirable person.

Narcissists will also lie and tell their victim that their friend, sister, mother or coworker also thinks they're crazy or hopeless, and this confuses the victim further, since they never got that impression from the third person when they were around them. This is another form of triangulation.

· Nitpicking

Nitpicking means continually finding faults in others and criticizing little things others do.

Narcissists are often perfectionists who want everything in life to turn out perfectly and so they are quick to find fault in people and things.

Are you a millionaire? The narcissist will then start to pick on you and ask you why you aren't a multi-millionaire yet.

At work, a narcissist will criticize you and say their motive is to help you improve and be the best, but they just want to nitpick and make you the scapegoat when things don't turn out well. Even when you meet their set targets, the narcissist will still find reasons to be dissatisfied with you.

When you argue with a narcissist, and you have presented all the evidence that could validate you, a narcissist will still demand more proof and bring in matters not relevant to the matter of contention. They do this by pointing out one irrelevant fact or one thing you did wrong and then change the whole direction of the argument.

Gaslighting narcissists will use these techniques to make their victims think that they are crazy. They do this in subtle ways you can't easily recognize, so it is hard to see what they are really up to.

Gradually, the effects of gaslighting start to set in on the victim, and the victim experiences cognitive dissonance, and after continuous gaslighting, the victim starts to question their sanity and think they are actually going crazy.

Chapter 5. How To Avoid Manipulation

In this section, we will talk about the different steps you can take to avoid being gaslighted. But before this, I must address those of you who are reading this book and experiencing abuse yourselves. If you are reading this book because you suspected that you were being gaslighted, or because you're feeling trapped in some kind of relationship, and you're finding out that some or all of the signs that are mentioned in the book sound familiar to you, please make sure to seek help. There is help available for you out there at violence shelters and with therapists. I strongly recommend that you talk openly to your friends or your family, to find a trusted person who will know what you're going through and will be your strength when things get harder. Acknowledging that there is a problem is the first step to healing.

Set boundaries

The first step is to set boundaries. It is important to state the boundary clearly, as well as the consequences for crossing that boundary, so that the gaslighter will correctly associate your response to his inappropriate actions. For example, you might tell him that you will no longer put up with an outburst of rage, and that, if he does blow up at you again, you will leave. When he does blow up again (and he probably will), you must follow through on your consequences. Leave. Go to a friend's house or a family member's place. You can decide the terms for when or if you will return. The important thing is to follow through on the consequences, or the gaslighter will never respect your boundaries.

Boundaries are there to protect you. Boundaries are going to protect you from a gaslighter because they keep you from the lies that the gaslighter is telling you. You can stand up for yourself and say "The next time that you make me feel stupid or useless, or you talk to me that way, I will leave this relationship permanently". This way, you will have a trigger to help you take the first step and move out. The ultimate boundary will be to completely remove yourself from that person's influence, break the relationship off and burn the bridge, and get the destructive person out of your life.

Focus on the truth

The second way to handle gaslighting is to focus on the truth. Don't get so caught up with trying to recognize the lies. Stop playing scenarios in your head. Become your own best friend and trust yourself.

Focus on the facts. Make sure to fight for your own truth also in situations that are not related to the gaslighter. Focus on the things that you know about yourself. Focus on the truth about what you have experienced and allow that to guide you.

Keep a journal

The third way to deal with gaslighting is to keep a record of your life. Record the deeds, needs, and times. Both important and not important. This will help you to recheck facts. In addition, it's proven that after something ends, we tend to remember mostly the positive things that have happened. During this period, it's easier to fall back into manipulation. A journal will help you to remember clearly and keep you strong.

Use the broken record technique

The next way to deal with gaslighting is the broken record technique. Use this when you are asking the person who is gaslighting you questions, such as where they were the night before. If you find that you're asking a simple question and they are not giving you an answer or they're trying to take the conversation on a tangent, or simply saying, "Oh, out," you should repeat your question. Keep on saying, "Where were you last night?" and if they say something like, "I sent you a message yesterday and you didn't answer it," keep on asking them "Where were you last night?" Continue to ask the same question over and over again "Where were you last night? Where were you last night?" like a broken record until they answer it.

This term comes from what a needle does to a record that gets scratched or broken in some way. The needle stays in the same groove and repeats the same piece over and over until you move it manually. You are waiting for the other person to actually answer you so that you can get what you need out of the conversation. You deserve the truth, and you need the truth.

Refuse to let the conversation be hijacked

When you noticed that a conversation or discussion is being hijacked down some tangent or other away from what you are trying to discuss, you can take a break and walk away from the conversation.

There is no point in your trying to argue your way back to your original topic. Let it go for that moment, put a pin in it and then at the next opportunity, like the next morning, when things are a little bit calmer, or the next evening, you can bring the topic up once again. If the person tries to delay it again, just tell him that you are not going to derail the conversation from something important to you. You need to have that conversation and not let them derail you. But you don't have to have that conversation with them when they are upset, especially if you are in a toxic relationship. You have the power to walk away for the moment, and return to it at a later time. You owe it to yourself to protect yourself from any form of gaslighting abuse.

Chapter 6. Gaslighting In Intimate Relationships

You read a message on your partner's phone, and you get that bad feeling that feels like a punch in the stomach. Did he really do it? Is he unfaithful? The message doesn't leave any doubt. You hope that you're wrong – you did everything in your power to make him love you – why isn't it enough? You approach him and you hear no real explanation. Instead, you're told that you misjudged the email; that you're overreacting. That you always lie and make things up. Your instincts say otherwise; but you may second-guess yourself enough to give in and believe the story your partner is telling you. "Maybe he's right. Maybe I am overreacting. Now he's mad at me. I shouldn't jump to conclusions like that."

This is a perfect example of gaslighting in a relationship, where one person makes the other question reality in order to gain control in the relationship. He also blames the other in order to make her feel guilty. The recurrence of these situations make you question your convictions and, in the end, lose your sense of discernment.

Being involved with a gaslighter is a form of mental abuse, and you have to remember that when it is happening, so that you don't get blindsided.

When you recognize the strategies that your partner uses, you will be able to leave the relationship before it causes irreparable harm.

35 Warning Signs of Gaslighting in a Relationship

1. You are regularly reminded of your weaknesses.

When your partner constantly reminds you of your shortcomings or faults, you begin to believe that you can never do anything right. The gaslighter doesn't use these reminders as a way to improve the relationship, but rather to make you feel inadequate. By making you feel hopeless, the gaslighter gains power in the relationship.

2. You feel insecure

If your spouse is gaslighting you, you are likely to be frequently unsure of yourself. You might be shaky about your habits, distrustful of your partner's thought processes, and anxious about their unpredictable reactions towards you.

3. You question your worth

You may begin to question your worth as an individual. You may wonder whether you really are a failure as a spouse, and a failure in your other relationships as well. Since your partner makes you feel as if your observations are wrong, you question your own judgment.

4. You always tread lightly

Those being gaslighted often feel like they can't talk openly to their spouses without being put down. They feel tense and on edge as they anticipate their partner mocking or dismissing them. In contrast, they feel increasingly free and sure during those rare times when they are away from their partners.

5. Your partner doesn't admit their own faults

Since a gaslighter is often in attack mode, they very rarely own up to their own faults or failings. If they are criticized, they rush to accuse others or rationalize their behavior. Even when reality is perfectly clear to you, a gaslighter will not admit you are right.

6. Your partner behaves like a victim when criticized

If you criticize a gaslighter, he will play the victim to cover up his failings, and attempt to redirect fault to you by making accusations and false claims. By doing this, the gaslighter takes the focus off of himself and gets away with his denials and deflections.

7. You make negative comments about yourself

Since your spouse questions your perceptions and character over and over again, you may begin to question yourself and internalize some of the gaslighter's allegations about you. You may even start to deny your own character and qualities and say things like, "I'm only a dolt. I'm bad at making choices".

8. You apologize a great deal

If your default reaction to everything is to apologize, this is a warning sign that you don't have a sense of security to talk about your reality.

9. You continually look for approval from the gaslighter

Despite being constantly put down, you continually seek the gaslighter's approval. You become more and more agreeable and compliant in the hopes of relieving the pressure and being treated better. Because the gaslighter can give approval, they can also withhold it.

10. You rationalize the gaslighter's conduct

A few unfortunate victims feel embarrassed about being weak in a relationship. They either go into denial and imagine all is well; or they make up excuses for their partner's conduct, telling others, "It's all my fault" or "I'm just too sensitive". Victims of this abuse have serious difficulty acknowledging and understanding what's really going on.

11. Your partner lies

You realize that your partner is lying, but she is saying it with a straight face. A gaslighter is just laying the groundwork for the future by doing this. Their objective is to make you feel insecure and crazy.

12. They deny something you have proof of

You are sure your partner said he would do something – you know beyond a doubt how the conversation went. Nevertheless, he adamantly denies it. This makes you start questioning what you know to be true, and wondering why your world is not the same as your partner's. The more this happens, the more you question your own perceptions and begin to accept his version without question.

13. They attack what is meaningful to you

Gaslighters know what is precious to their partners and use these things in their attacks. For instance, your partner may know how important your child is to you, so your parenting skills might be one of the primary things they attack. They may tell you that you should never even have had a child because you are such a horrible parent. You might begin to believe them even if deep down you know it's not true.

14. They wear you down, bit by bit

A gaslighter does his work step by step. A lie here, a slightly inconsiderate remark there, and usually without your being able to pinpoint it. Indeed, even the most mindful individuals can be sucked into the gaslighter's abuse without realizing it, since it is so subtle.

15. They don't do what they say

Their actions don't line up with their words, so what they say means nothing.

16. They throw you off with bits of praise

The person who continually cuts you down suddenly applauds you for something. This makes you feel confused, and you begin to wonder if your partner is truly as terrible as you have suspected. This is meant to keep you off balance, to control you, and to make you question your world.

17. When you do get praise, it's for something that benefitted your partner

Think about what you did to earn a couple of seconds of recognition. Was it something that benefitted your partner somehow? Does the praise go along with when you do what your partner wants? If this is true, it is simply one more form of gaslighting, since you don't get praised for the things that really matter to you.

18. They try to confuse you

Gaslighters know that people like to feel strong. They try to undermine this and make you question everything. During this time of insecurity, you look for someone who can help you make sense of your life and give you a sense of security, which, unfortunately, is often the gaslighter. This turns into an endless cycle of torment and confusion.

19. They anticipate your criticism of their bad behavior

They undermine you, yet constantly blame you for being the con artist. They lie relentlessly yet condemn you for being a liar. This happens so often that you spend all of your time trying to defend yourself and are distracted from your partner's conduct. That is what your partner wants.

20. They use other people against you

Gaslighters know who will support them no matter what, and they try to make you feel like these people don't care about you. They will say, "My mother has no doubt about it". "Even my closest friends don't like you". Remember that these statements might never have been really said. As a steady liar, the gaslighter uses this strategy to make you feel like you can't trust anybody.

21. They isolate you

The gaslighter isolates you by making you question who you can trust, and by becoming the only one available to you. This isolation gives them control over you. The perceived rejection by others turns into a wound, and the only person you can turn to is the one tormenting you.

22. They tell others that you are crazy

This makes others question your mental stability. Other people will have a hard time believing you when you say that the gaslighter is abusing you.

23. They insist that everyone else is lying

By telling you that everyone else is lying, they make you question your own facts. This makes you turn to them for the 'truth', which is, in fact, a lie.

24. You begin to wonder if you are too sensitive

You've never thought that you were overly sensitive before, but now that you are being told constantly that you are, you begin to wonder if it's true, which it is definitely not. But the damage is done: you begin to believe that you can't say anything, because you're overreacting.

25. You wonder why you are so upset

You have so many good things in your life, you wonder why you feel so distressed. Why have you gone from being a happy person to always feeling anxious now that you are in this new relationship? This might be because of your partner's abuse.

26. You start to lie to your partner to avoid being put down

You start to recognize when a confrontation or put-down is coming, and you lie or avoid a discussion altogether just to avoid the insults.

27. You being to struggle with making basic choices in your relationship

Maybe you and your spouse are going out to dinner, and you are picking the spot. You may stress excessively over where to go, for fear of making the wrong decision and being criticized for not choosing what your partner wanted.

28. You feel defeated

You begin to feel like there is nothing you can do right, so you are totally crushed. This will cause you to agree with anything and everything your partner says, which is their objective.

29. Your spouse contradicts everything you say

Do you often end up saying, "Goodness, I thought you said…." Only to have your spouse insist that you are wrong? If they continually make you question your memory of events and conversations, that is a major red flag. This strategy is often used to create confusion and doubt, and hide things that they know aren't right.

30. You trust someone else's judgment more than your own

Your spouse makes you question what is or isn't normal in a relationship. He may say things like, "Every couple fights like we do", or "You don't have the foggiest idea of what a solid relationship looks like". So you often question your own judgment and feel that other people are smarter than you are.

31. You stop trusting yourself

You stop trusting yourself and trusting your own choices. You accept that whatever choice you make will be the wrong one.

32. You feel as if something is 'off'

You will most likely not be able to put your finger on it, but your gut is telling you that something isn't right. You may even be hesitant to let it be known or talk to other people about it.

33. You lose your sense of identity

It's not unusual to be insecure if you are in an abusive relationship like this. Both partners are insecure; however the partner being controlled has a greater sense of insecurity than their partner's. The unfortunate victim loses their identity and takes on the personality given to them by their partner.

34. Your vitality is depleted

Being in this sort of relationship will drain you of your vitality, because you invest so much energy into worrying about what to say and do that won't be attacked. You will feel continually drained from pouring so much energy into your partner.

35. Your partner doesn't try to do what they say other people should do

When you are in a relationship with a gaslighter, it might be hard to understand their thought processes. You may have a discussion with them where they sound understanding and caring. But when you live with them, they act in a different way. They may tell you that they love you, but they do things that hurt you. Know that gaslighters are best understood by watching what they do, not listening to what they say.

How to Address Gaslighting in a Relationship

At their core, gaslighters are cynics, and they will never take a good, hard look at themselves. If they've harmed or annoyed you and you react, they tell you that you're oversensitive or tend to blow up. But in reality, they are the ones who are oversensitive and blow up over nothing. With that in mind, we'll handle how to react to gaslighting by separating it into eight stages — which are all basic to your successful recovery, and to protecting yourself as well from other gaslighters.

Understand the gaslighter's strategies.

Recognize the particular strategies the gaslighter in your life uses and call them what they are. Recall how the gaslighter first made you question what you saw or what it meant to you. The gaslighter doesn't simply question your objective facts; they also attack the significance of what you may have seen. In this way, if they can't convince you that "it never happened," they'll work at persuading you that "it is not a big deal, anyway," and "no doubt about it." Identify the gaslighter's preferred strategies, call them by name, and choose stop making excuses for your abuser.

Remember who you were before you met the gaslighter.

Recall how you lived, what you appreciated, and what you were like around other people — especially those close to you.

48

List the characteristics you like about the person you used to be. Are you the same person you used to be or do you seem different?

It's entirely normal to think about the things you do not like about that person, too. We're every one of us a work in progress.

In any case, for the time being, focus on the characteristics you like and need to recreate or put to use.

The issue isn't you. Furthermore, you can get yourself back — if you want to.

Choose what sort of individual you need to be (and whose!).

Choose who you need to be for an amazing life and how you will need to continue developing.

Choose who will drive that development and who will eventually be answerable for the decisions you make.

All things considered, *you* are the person who needs to live with yourself; however, you're not by any means the only one who suffers when you cling to a harmful relationship.

Your example influences a larger number of people than you know.

Once you've thought about who you are now, who you used to be, and who you want to be — free of and separated from the gaslighter — go on to the next stage.

What steps you can take to be that person:

Now, ask yourself some hard questions:

Do I need to make a total separation from this individual, or is it realistically possible to change them?

Is it conceivable that, after we separate, the gaslighter will change their ways?

Will I be able to be the person I want to be and remain in this relationship?

49

What sort of person does the gaslighter need me to be?

What will it cost me to remain with this individual — and what will it cost to leave?

You need space and opportunity out from under someone else's control to explore the person you want to be, and to develop in that direction. As long as somebody is trying to control you and keep you heading in a different direction, the best you can do is simply stagnate. Since each incidence of a gaslighter's abuse robs you of fundament al vitality, you have to separate to become your true self and the better person you want to be.

Are you prepared to break free, regardless of whether it hurts? Then it's time to have a discussion with the gaslighter to inform them of your decision. Here are some guidelines for that discussion:

Enlist the support of steady, reliable loved ones.

Prepare what you will say.

Schedule the discussion so your support person (or people) can be there with you or ready nearby. Stage it on neutral ground, so the gaslighter won't have you off-guard. You'll need to make sure that this individual can't use their size, their voice, or the threat of violence to quiet, disgrace, or threaten you. Be ready to act on your decision, as well. If you've been living with the gaslighter, you ought to have just moved your belongings to more safe place (ideally a place that the gaslighter won't think about). If you're living alone, request that somebody remain with you that night.

Confront the gaslighter on neutral ground:

Pick a spot where you have a sense of security — a spot that evens the odds. Try not to let the gaslighter control you into meeting where they have the upper hand (for example, your shared home, or their place). While you would prefer not to put the gaslighter on edge, it's totally sensible to pick the place yourself so as to guarantee you can't be intimidated (verbally or physically).

It's possible for the gaslighting abuse to turn into physical abuse. If somebody is happy to make you feel little, frail, and powerless, they're also presumably ready to use physical power if a verbal outburst isn't enough to hold you under their influence.

Make a complete separation.

After stating what you have to say – before the gaslighter responds— say goodbye and let them realize the relationship is finished. You know you can't be the person you need to be and remain in the relationship, so you're doing what you know is best for both of you and won't be bullied into changing your mind.

Because the gaslighter will use any means of communication to try to manipulate you into a position of reliance and weakness again, state clearly that you don't want any communication at all from this person — no calls, no writing, no messages, nothing. If they send roses or some other gift, it will wind up in the trash or be given to another person. You don't need anything more from them, and you would prefer not to see them again.

Give yourself a couple of months to recuperate from the relationship before you start dating once more. Furthermore, when you do begin meeting new people, be on the lookout for gaslighting practices. Don't let yourself get close to somebody who causes alarm bells to go off in your mind. You quieted these alarms before, and you could do so once again. We, as a whole, can. It's something we do over and over again to keep from something we consider to be a miserable outcome: winding up alone. But there are worse things than spending a long time single and unattached — as you acknowledged before choosing to say a final farewell to the gaslighter. Remind yourself you deserve better. May your genuineness and new-found strength impact all that you do today.

Chapter 7. Gaslighting In the Work-Place

Narcissists tend to be bullies, and they enjoy it. So if you have a narcissist coworker, then you will observe that person likes bullying other people. They will act as if they were your boss, even when they are not. They might ask you to do things that are below your pay grade. They will ask you to file papers when you're an award-winning certified public accountant. They might even try to raise their voice at you. They might suggest that you did things that you didn't do. They might lie about you. They might shout at you. They might call you names. They might steal things from you. They might talk about you behind your back. They might steal your lunch from the refrigerator and when you catch them, they will tell you flat out that it is not your lunch. Whatever way they express it, the goal is the same: to make you lose self-confidence.

How a Narcissist will Undermine Your Self-Confidence

First, they engage in sexual harassment

If you work with somebody who is a narcissist, then chances ar you will experience sexual harassment in addition to bullying, because narcissists lack empathy for others and will always want to exploit other people.

They don't actually see other people as valued members of society who have feelings. They love to exploit other people when it comes to sexual harassment and they are more likely to do it. There is a link between narcissism and sexual harassment. Heads of major corporations and some music moguls have been in the news recently, having been accused and convicted of sexual harassment. So if you work with someone who makes comments about your coworkers' looks and bodies, or who shames people about their looks, they are most likely narcissistic people.

They exploit you for their own gain

Narcissists tend to exploit other people for their own gain, to boost their sense of superiority. This happens whether they are in a position of authority or not - they are still going to exploit people. They will constantly stroke your ego so that you appreciate them fully. As long as you continue to play the game, they will be on good terms with you. But the minute that you challenge them, they are going feel slighted by you. The minute they realize that you have figured them out, they will be on the warpath.

A work relationship with a narcissist will be "on" one day and "off" the next. There is simply no middle ground for them: they either love you or hate you. Either they ignore you or they try to pull you down. They might be friends with you one day, but the minute that you have an off day where you don't feed their ego, they will turn on you. More importantly, the moment that they feel that you are making some headway in the company

- they will start to feel threatened by you. If you impress the boss, a narcissist will see that as a threat. Anytime they feel that they are losing their power over you, or their feeling of power over you, you will see the ugly side of their personality.

They exaggerate their own importance

Narcissists continually boast about their accomplishments at work. In reality, they are so unproductive and you can see right through them, but they want you to believe that they are incredibly productive and that they are highly valuable to the company. They keep boasting about what they did and didn't do. They might happen to meet the CEO briefly in the parking lot, but then come back the next day, and brag that they had lunch with him! They exaggerate who they are and they want you to believe it. They want you to be sucked into their fantasy world and they do it because they are so insecure and they think that this is the way they will gain your respect.

You will also see them enter in the middle of a conversation and redirect the attention on themselves. They will then monopolize the conversation.

In order to fully exploit all the people in the office, and feel a sense of superiority, they like to be known as the ones that get easily upset so anyone should be working around them walking on eggshells.

Narcissists turn into gaslighters when they never admit to a mistake. In fact, they will make up every excuse in the world to blame someone else for something they did that fell apart, or something they were responsible for that was not done.

They refuse to take responsibility and blame whoever is in the room. They most often pick the person that doesn't fight them back. They will lie about their own shortcomings and take it out on somebody in the office whom they feel won't fight back or whom they feel will back down.

That is why it's very important that you have boundaries. They keep gaslighters at bay. This is a huge part of the recovery process.

They take credit for your work

One of the most difficult aspects of these people is that they tend to take credit for your work. They are ones sitting back and bothering you - asking you for information about your project and asking you how far along with it you are. They might even buy you coffee and support you so that you can complete the project. Then they take credit for it in front of your boss. This really speaks to their inability to care about other people authentically. The agenda is always to maintain power over the people that they are working with. It is their agenda to control, manipulate and dominate other people, and you will find it very destructive to try to work on a team with a narcissist. They will always steal the credit for your work without an ounce of remorse.

What Should You Do if Someone is Gaslighting You at Work?

If you feel as though someone is gaslighting you at work, there are several steps you can take to keep your distance from the damaging person.

Here are my recommendations:

1. Educate yourself about gaslighting.

Gaslighters are very good at ramping up their manipulative behavior slowly. The more you know about the manipulation tactics gaslighters use, the more quickly you can spot them.

2. Identify the Perpetrator's Behavior Patterns

Look out for patterns that try to confuse you. If a boss, coworker, subordinate or someone else in the workplace is consistently trying to confuse you and make you question your own trust in yourself and your perceptions of reality, consider the fact that they might be gaslighting you.

3. Trust Your Gut

After you understand what's going on, realize that this might be because of their own shame over something they've done wrong (and refuse to accept blame for) or their own insecurities at work, and do not take on their shame or insecurities as your own. Stand your ground by putting your foot down. Don't let the gaslighter's words or actions affect you or your work. If you're really questioning your sanity, ask another coworker to vouch for you or step in so they can give you their input as well. If a coworker was there, for example, when your boss promised a raise but later denied it, talk to that coworker to provide some level of proof that you're not as crazy as your boss has made you feel.

4. Write it all Down

If you have to, write down what you believe to be true. Write down situations as they happen, so when you feel as though you're a victim of gaslighting, you can refer back to your own real-time accounts of the situation.

5. Consciously Affirm Your Own Value

Remind yourself that your work is valuable, and you are valued. Remember that you are worthy and professional, that there was a reason this company hired you in the first place, and that there's a reason you haven't been fired.

6. Talk to the Perpetrator

Let your gaslighter know that you're aware of what's going on — let them know that you have proof that they're spreading falsehoods or putting false information into your head, and let it be known that you're not affected by it. Talk to them gently to help them come out of denial. Know your workplace's guidelines (or lack thereof) about reporting harassment. Large companies may have a policy that harassment complaints are reported to the Human Resources department. Smaller companies may not have a plan in place.

7. But Don't Confront Them Directly!

If the gentle approach does not work, do not become confrontational with them. Gaslighters respond to criticism with personal attacks: they'll feel threatened by any direct challenge and retaliate. They may even accuse you of gaslighting them. So as much as you can, try to avoid contact. Instead, consult HR for strategies on minimizing your time with them. After all, that's what they're paid for!

8. Prepare for A Struggle—And Leave If You Have To

Gaslighters thrive on our desire for approval and fear of abandonment. And as much as they piss you off, you try to please them and fear their rejection. So, prepare to second-guess yourself as you break away from their web. And if necessary, leave your job. Your sanity and self-worth are worth more than a salary or someone else's approval.

The effects of gaslighting on the employee

Gaslighting can take an otherwise high-functioning individual and turn them into a low performer who eventually leaves the team, company, and even industry. This is because, over time, the target or targets of gaslighting experience:

Loss of motivation

Loss of self-esteem

Stagnation of career progression

Loss of ability to make decisions

Anxiety and/or depression, which can eventually lead to physical illness and/or PTSD

Gaslighting and diversity and inclusion

While gaslighting can impact anyone, it is more likely to impact people from underrepresented groups, and the adverse effects on these individuals are often more severe. Gaslighting is particularly effective when there's an imbalance in power, and underrepresented versus overrepresented groups create an implicit power dynamic.

Chapter 8. Signs That You're Being Manipulated With Gaslighting

Although gaslighting is emotional bullying and should be obvious, many people are unsure of what a gaslighter looks like or if they are victims of gaslighting. One reason for this confusion is that gaslighters have a way of shutting their victims up with overt or covert threats because of a real or perceived power imbalance or mismatch. But it doesn't have to be that way. It is really not difficult to recognize a gaslighter, neither is it rocket science to pinpoint a victim of gaslighting as you will discover in this chapter.

Gaslighting in Men and Women

Gaslighting in Men

As unbelievable as it may sound to some people, a good number of men are victims of domestic violence, including gaslighting. The notion that men are always the abusers and not the abused comes from the idea that men are physically stronger than women and are not as emotional as women. Also, many people assume that domestic or emotional abuse always means physical abuse. Indeed emotional abuse, and gaslighting in particular, can be a precursor to physical violence, but that is not always the case. Some gaslighters can be very charming and put on an appearance of being weak, vulnerable and harmless, but then execute the most deadly form of emotional abuse. Men can also be gaslighted by other male friends and colleagues in the workplace and other settings, too. However, in this section, the focus will be more on men who are gaslighted by their female partners.

Perhaps you know a man who always makes these excuses for his spouse's bad behavior:

"She is just being moody because things are a bit rough."

"She's having an emotional outburst."

"She is strong-willed."

He may be hiding something about the situation in his relationship. It is not surprising for men to refuse to acknowledge psychological abuse, especially from a female partner, because of the general ideas about masculinity. Men may hesitate to mention that they are victims of gaslighting by a woman because of the possible scorn that they will face. It is generally easier to believe that a woman is the victim of gaslighting or that a man is gaslighted by another man (his boss, friend, or colleague). But that doesn't mean that men don't face these challenges.

Spotting the Male Victim

Generally, men who suffer gaslighting can suddenly change their contact patterns, demeanor, and work behavior. But here are some more specific telltale signs that a man you know could be a victim of gaslighting or even other forms of emotional abuse:

- A man who is excessively anxious to please his partner.

- A man who has a deep fear of upsetting his spouse.

- A man who frequently reports his whereabouts and what he is doing to his female partner.

- A man who always agrees with everything his spouse says and does.

- A man who is constantly harassed by phone calls from his spouse.

- A man who suffers from parental alienation—having his children turned against him by their mother.

• A sudden decline in a man's hygiene and physical appearance (from smart to unkempt).

• A man who suddenly starts drinking or increases his alcohol consumption. Or a man who resorts to using hard drugs.

• A man who constantly looks unwell or exhausted.

• A man who frequently absents himself from work or social occasions with no concrete reasons.

Bottom line: If you suspect that a man is a victim of gaslighting, do not blame or judge him and don't expect him to come to you about it. Men usually don't like to share their feelings but by bearing that in mind and by creating an environment of trust and acceptance, you might get them to open up and ask for help . Listen to them and validate their concerns and don't start pestering them with unsolicited advice. Express concern about their mental well-being and persuade them to seek help. Share some stories of other men who had similar negative experiences so they see that they are not alone. If you are a man who is being gaslighted (either by a woman or another man), I strongly recommend that you religiously apply the suggestions in this book.

Gaslighting in Women

Women are persuaded into believing that their perception of reality is somehow unreliable and shouldn't be trusted. Women are often reminded that "It's a man's world," so they should listen to men regardless of whether they are right or wrong.

But a healthy professional relationship is one where both partners care about each other's feelings and concerns. If a man constantly dismisses, belittles or takes a woman's concerns lightly, it is a sign that he doesn't genuinely value her. If a man always finds a way to shift the blame on you, particularly because you are a woman, he is likely gaslighting you.

Spotting the Female Victim

It is easier to spot a woman who is being gaslighted than a man. Here are the more common warning signs:

- A woman who is afraid of standing up or speaking up for herself.

- A woman who is hardly ever seen in public without her male partner.

- A woman who has limited access to the car, cash, and credit cards.

- A woman who has no access to social media, or limited access to friends and family.

- A woman who has frequent injuries and tries to cover it up with the lame excuse, "It was an accident."

Dead Giveaways

The first step to rid yourself of something you don't want is to identify that exact thing. Dealing with gaslighting is no different. If you are not sure whether you are being gaslighted in your professional or personal relationship, then I invite you to study the clues that follow. However, one thing you should never ignore is your gut—trust it because if you are feeling that something is off about someone, it probably is.

But first, be aware that it is never your fault if someone gaslights you. Gaslighting doesn't happen because you are naïve, weak, immature, or inadequate. Gaslighting is never about the victim's shortcomings but about the abuser's malicious intent. The gaslighter may have had a rough past, a difficult upbringing, or could be suffering from a disorder—Narcissistic Personality Disorder (NPD). Whatever the case, the gaslighter is also a victim of their past and environment, or victim of a mental disorder. They also need help, fast!

Now, let's go into the details of how to identify a gaslighter, regardless of gender. Keep in mind that some of the warning signs below may be exhibited by people who are not emotional abusers. What you are looking for is a pattern of behavior and not one-off occurrences or instances of these behaviors. If someone you know consistently shows enough of these signs, you may be dealing with a gaslighter.

1.   Unfair Comparisons

Gaslighters use comparison as a weapon to pit people against each other. In the workplace, they will always bring up a very unrealistic comparison between two people's performances, even when their jobs are unrelated, just to create unhealthy competition. A gaslighting parent will often have a special or golden child who is always right no matter what they do and another child who is always wrong no matter how hard they try to do right. To make matters worse, they often rub the 'rightness' of the golden child in the face of the never-do-good child. This can lead to a lifelong rivalry between the siblings. If you are in an intimate relationship with a gaslighter, they may often compare you to their ex or someone else. To them, you are never as good as some other person, no matter how hard you try.

2.   Divide and Conquer

Closely related to the unfair comparison warning sign is the divide and conquer. But instead of using comparison to pit people against each other, the gaslighter peddles lies, spreads malicious rumors, or says damning things behind other people's backs to get them to distrust each other. For example, they can say something like, "You haven't heard? The whole department/family/school is talking about you. They think you can't hold it together." They can make a mutual friend believe that you said unflattering things about them and then take pleasure from seeing you argue with the other person. In some cases, the gaslighter can make a show of negotiating 'peace' to end the conflict that they masterminded to begin with. The goal is simple: to get you to trust <u>them</u> so that they can control your opinion about the mutual friend. Meanwhile, they are likely to do the same thing with the other friend. These types of gaslighters are the 'perfect' schemers—they get people to distrust each other so that they can trust them.

3.   Telling Outright Lies

There is no such thing as catching a gaslighter in the act of telling a lie because they will boldly deny it. Other people may try to wriggle out of a lie by muttering some excuses but not a gaslighter; they will tell you point-blank that they are not guilty of your accusations. This can result in self-doubt—you may begin to question how sure you were of your accusations. Questioning your version of reality and relying on theirs is one of the main goals of the gaslighter. And they use outright lies to achieve that.

4.   Conditional Apologies

Conditional apologies (also known as non-apology apology) are not apologies at all. They are tools that gaslighters use to manipulate you into thinking that they are sorry for something that they have said or done wrong. But if you still feel that something is off after the so-called apology, it is because something _is_ off. They didn't offer an apology. What they did was to move on prematurely after making excuses, avoiding responsibility, downplaying their wrong deeds, shifting blame, confusing, or invalidating you. Also, if you have to demand an apology before you get it, the person making the apology probably doesn't mean it. They are just doing something to get you off their backs.

There are several ways gaslighters use conditional apologies. A few of these are:

• A limited apology or an apology that includes a conditional modifier. For example, "I am sorry if I hurt your feelings."

• Blame-shifting apology. For example, "I am sorry you found my comments offensive."

• Bullying apology. For example, "Oh give me a break, I am sorry, okay?"

• Justifying apology. For example, "I was just kidding."

• Excuse-making apology. For example, "I am sorry, but it was largely your fault."

- Déjà-vu apology. For example, "I already apologized before!"

- No-need-to-apologize apology. For example, "You know I would not hurt you intentionally."

Gaslighters always want to be in control. A genuine apology will dislodge them from that position of control, so they would rather offer a conditional apology to sidestep taking responsibility for their behavior and remain in control.

5.   Unreciprocated Loyalty

Gaslighters expect other people to be 100% loyal to them. But they are hardly loyal to anyone. For example, in intimate or romantic relationships, they are known for their high level of infidelity. Worst still, they don't apologize even when they are caught with their pants down. They will either lie outright ("Nothing happened. You're just overreacting!"), or offer some conditional apology ("I'm sorry, but you pushed me into this mess!").

6 .   Isolation

One way gaslighters maintain control over their victims is to isolate them from the important people in their lives. They can do this covertly or overtly. When someone in your life constantly complains that you don't spend enough time with them (even when you do), they may be trying to craftily isolate you from others. They will gripe and whine about how you spend too much time with your family members, your friends, or colleagues. They will always remind you how lonely and boring it gets when you are not around. They may even make unreasonable requests, such as telling you that they love you and would want to spend every waking moment of their lives with you! A person who tells you that your family makes them uncomfortable or gives some flimsy excuse for not meeting your family may be secretly trying to keep you away from them to spend more time alone together.

Overt isolation can be in the form of unreasonable choices, such as making you choose between them and other people. It can also be an ultimatum. For example, "If you ever go to see them again, it's over between us!"

Other people in your life (good friends, supportive colleagues, and family) are your social network who can provide strong moral, emotional, and financial support. The gaslighter will try to cut you off from your network so that you will have to depend on them for almost everything.

7.   Avoiding Personal Responsibility

A gaslighter is always right! In their opinion, there is nothing wrong with their behavior, but everyone else's behavior is faulty. As long as what they do is in line with their ego, it is all good and fine. This can be linked to what is called an egosyntonic personality disorder that makes those with the disorder think that everyone else is crazy except them. It is usually difficult to treat someone with this type of disorder. If someone you know always shifts blame, points accusing fingers or never accepts personal responsibility even when they are as guilty as sin, he or she may be an egosyntonic gaslighter.

8.   Discrediting Others

Gaslighters can tell others to "tread lightly" around you because you are "losing it." They will paint you black before others to discredit you. They will make others see you as unstable or fragile. If someone is always telling others to be careful around you, they may be gaslighting you.

9 .   Expecting Special Treatment

Gaslighters tend to assume that they should get special treatment and when they don't get it, they can become irrationally angry. For example, a gaslighting husband may expect his wife to have dinner ready at a particular time. If she doesn't meet up with this expectation for whatever reason, the gaslighting husband can become furious and even retaliate in some way. A gaslighting wife can become excessively demanding of her husband and fly into a rage if the man can't meet her demands.

What Next?

So, you've recognized some of these signs in someone and you're sure they are gaslighting you. What next? Here's something you can do right away. Walk away from any relationship, friendship, or partnership that you can end without any complications. If it is a relationship that you're deeply involved in emotionally, it may be a bit challenging to just up and go. The rest of this book will explain in detail the necessary steps you can take to free yourself from this person's attack and to protect yourself from further abuse.

Chapter 9. Secret Manipulation Tactics

Abusers aren't unintelligent people—many of them are very smart, which enables them to understand how to manipulate you and how efficiently they can do so while still keeping you around. However, the way that they do it is very simple. These tactics, at their core, are easily deflected and you can protect yourself against them every single time if you're able to trust your gut and understand what you're looking for. In general, the tactics of an abuser are based on the emotions of the victim and the lack thereof on the part of the abuser. While this can seem very cruel on their part, they do understand the emotions of others to a literal extent. They don't understand their own emotions sometimes. They don't understand how the emotions of other people apply to them or how they can actually connect with people genuinely.

The main defense mechanism that a victim can use to their advantage is eliminating the element of surprise. This is what the abuser uses to pull the rug out from under their victim every single time they pull them back in with their charisma. In short, stop wondering what to expect—expect what to wonder. Being able to react quickly to potentially abusive and dangerous situations empowers you to act in a way you might not have been able to if you had no clue of what was happening around you. Being perceptive and becoming used to the tactics of your abuser can and will help you get out of that relationship. Abusers tend to follow some kind of pattern, and they fall back on these patterns more often than not. So, look for these cycles of behaviors and track them, and a way out will become apparent.

In addition to understanding why the tactics work in general, you have to understand why they work on you in particular. Most abusers pick their victims for a reason. Many abusers know how to pick out an empath or someone else who's suffered trauma in the past. Think about what part of your personality leaves you open to being taken advantage of. This doesn't mean that you should ever assume that the abuse is your fault. But you should always be considering how you can be more careful in the future – for your own sake. Being able to protect yourself not only from this abuse but from the possibility of abuse like this in the future keeps you safe and aware. Many victims fall into the "this time will be different" mentality and allow their optimism to override their sense of logic, pulling them back into the cycle of abuse with a different emotional manipulator. There are many tactics itn this list that your abuser has never used because they just might not work on you so well. Others, you may know far too well for comfort—because that particular tactic is especially effective on you for whatever reason. As you read, put yourself in the shoes of the collective "you" and consider what those reasons might be.

The first tactic that abusers use might be the most all-encompassing. All abusers will try to guilt you into feeling as though a bad relationship is your fault, even if there's no reasonable way this could be true. Simply put, this way of pushing guilt and shame onto the victim forces them into submission and makes them much more likely to stick around. The abuser makes up some narrative in which the fault truly lies with the victim and they should feel guilty. The victim often doesn't really have a way to stick up for themselves or argue back, so they simply take the blame.

For example, a date might go sour or the couple may fight for a long time one night. In reality, it might be that the abuser was at fault for the fight or whatever ruined the date. Or, there might have been no reason at all—just bad luck or a culmination of unfortunate circumstances. However, the abuser will try to make the victim feel as though it's their fault that these things happen, or that the victim could have prevented them. When this issue crops up in the middle of a fight or in your own relationship, take a step back and try to think your own way through the story. Don't automatically accept the way your partner sees it as the truth. Accept your own narrative before theirs.

Abusers will often try to force an answer or solution out of the victim when there isn't one. There may be a problem with a colleague at work, with a family member, or in some other relationship, and the two people involved might be at a complete loss. The abuser can't stand not being in control of whatever's happening at any given moment, and has a sense of urgency in having immediate answers to any issue they face. They'll often try to get their answers from their victim if they can't find them on their own. They'll try to push you to answer something or give a solution to a problem you can't solve. Even though they might know you don't have the required knowledge or time to solve the problem, they will keep pushing you to find a solution and they'll blame you for not finding one.

This kind of behavior makes many victims feel frustrated, and it increases the feeling of inferiority and incompetence. The need to please the abuser, combined with the sense of guilt that the abuser instills, is lethal for the person's sense of self-confidence. This leaves the victim wanting to do whatever he can to make the narcissist happy again. Being able to calmly deny requests you can't fulfill is an important part in the process of healing.

Most abusers are relatively petty in the way that they interact with their victims once they're upset. They often involve someone else to do the communicating for them. They cut themselves off from the victim and reinforce the feeling that whatever the miscommunication was originally about is the victim's fault. This is called triangulation—someone else is brought into a fight between a couple and communicates for one side as a third party.

Think back to a fight you might have had with your significant other, when they had a friend "talk" to you about it. This is an example of triangulation, and it works on most victims because it makes them feel cut off from their partner. When the abuser refuses to speak to their victim and work things out in a normal and healthy way, the victim is made to feel more alone than they did previously. It can be very difficult to work through that feeling and actually understand when something is the abuser's fault, and it usually takes some practice. If you see your partner trying to use a third party to communicate with you, refuse to indulge them. Only agree to speak to your partner—it isn't anybody else's business what you were fighting about, and your partner needs to understand that.

Your abuser loves to play the victim card whenever they see the chance. This is the underlying root of a lot of different manipulation tactics. The classic abuser knows how to take advantage of almost every situation and turn it on its head so that you look like the bad guy. If they can make it seem not only to other people, but to you, that you're somehow an antagonist or even abusive yourself, they win. Imagine you're having some kind of fight, and your partner begins firing everything you've ever done wrong to them at you. Every time you fought back against them; they spin into you having started the fight. But if you look for help apart from them, then they will spin it as betraying them or even being promiscuous.

They know how to get inside your head and under your skin, and how they can mess with your perception of yourself and the relationship. Understand that you cannot ever accept their narrative over your own. Ask other people who you trust and who support you about anything that's been going on and listen to the way they see things. Getting other people's opinions can help you form a more clear-headed narrative of the relationship, and you can get the power dynamic back.

When you feel like you're teetering on the edge of finally deciding to leave your abuser and abandon the relationship for your own sake, your abuser might try to pull you back in with their love-bombing tactics.

Love-bombing is a tactic I've touched on before, where the abuser will almost harass you with praise and love and shows of affection until you start to become infatuated with them again. The way that an abuser will love-bomb you varies from person to person, but most of them will either be very showy, or very gentle. Showy love-bombing includes things like public displays of affection and loudly declaring feelings for you. This puts social pressure on you, on top of the obligation you might feel toward them individually. You feel more compelled to accept and forgive when you're surrounded by onlookers.

71

More gentle love-bombing acknowledges and laments the decaying sense of connection and intimacy between the two of you—genuine sentiment and handholding are signs of gentle love-bombing. They're meant to get you back on their side and flood your system with the dopamine you experienced when you first met them so that you feel the relationship is able to be salvaged.

As a victim, be careful when your abuser suddenly starts to get incredibly nice to you seemingly out of nowhere. Be aware that there can be plenty of reasons for the sudden change of heart, some of them malicious.

Another way of playing the victim your abuser will often use is to try to get some kind of pity out of you. When you fight or almost separate, they'll do everything they can to remind you that they've also endured abuse, just like you. They'll do everything in their power to make themselves look like someone broken and hurt, just another victim of the cruel world around them. They know this works because they know just how empathetic you are, just how willing you are to back down and risk your own happiness for them. They know that and they're more than willing to take advantage of that.

They handpicked you because of your kindness, your ability to connect with others in a much more intimate and personal way. Because they know how much you can connect with them, especially as another victim of trauma, they also know they can get a lot of pity out of you. They know that you'll see them as someone broken, someone who needs help just like you do, and they know you'll try to help them, even if it means staying with them and being knowingly unhappy. If you see your abuser start to withdraw and they seem to become sadder or moping around you, keep this in mind—everything they do is to manipulate your feelings. Be wary of every emotion they express in your presence.

On the flip side of your abuser's emotional spectrum, they might notice that the softer side of their feelings isn't quite working on you. So, they might try to simply intimidate you into agreeing with them or staying with them. They know that they have to keep you at their side at all costs, so they'll limit where you can go and when, with whom, for how long. They have the means to limit these things and they'll know where you are. The obsessive traits of the abuser know no bounds, and they'll usually have some way to track you and know where you are so they can monitor your behavior and who you're hanging around with.

This intimidation usually comes in the wake of self-pity they feel from some wave of sadness that they expressed to you. They might notice that you aren't paying as much attention to them and their antics, so they'll switch their emotions to make you more afraid to resist or run away. They'll hide this intimidation behind an act of "love," or they'll claim to just want to keep you as safe as possible. If you see this happening, don't let your abuser bully you into believing it. Understand that you have to keep yourself safe but maintain your convictions and know that you are the victim of their abuse, not the other way around. This intimidation is not love, it's harassment.

To go right along with these methods of intimidation, many abusers will plainly bully and harass their victims into submission. They understand what makes their victims afraid of them and why they're afraid of other people—they understand much about their victim and use all the intimate understanding they have of them to their advantage. This includes not only the kind of intimidation that presents itself more discreetly but also plain bullying and verbal harassment. This is where intimidation really becomes abuse for the victim, and they're driven into a place where they feel forced to submit. The key thing about this particular method of abuse and manipulation is that the victim might feel as though they have to fight back, that they have to stand up for themselves or the abuse will only become worse.

In reality, the situation is usually made worse when the victim tries to fight back. If you are undergoing this abusive treatment, you must understand that there are ways to resist your abuser and fight back that don't necessarily involve physically fighting with them. Don't make it obvious— your resistance to their manipulation should be quiet and discreet. This way, you have a better chance of getting out without them noticing. Your priority should be your own safety, and that means you have to lay low on their radar from time to time.

As petty as most abusers are, it's the simplest and most petty methods of bullying that can get to you the most easily. Many abusers simply revert to being accusatory, calling their partner names and trying to demean them, making them feel as small and defenseless as possible. This name-calling might start off slow and small—during a fight, your abuser might suddenly call you a name or use a phrase that they know really affects you. They apologize, and you forgive them. But it keeps happening more and more as time goes on. Every fight you have, they call you names and verbally abuse you with nicknames and terms that make your blood boil. They're trying to get a rise out of you.

If you do react verbally to them, they know how they can get you off balance and surprise you. If they know how to rile you up, they also know how to force you into submission. This is just another way that the abuser tries to shift the power balance and keep it on their side for as long as possible. If you are seeing this happen between you and your partner right now, make sure that you can control your feelings; don't let them get an emotional reaction out of you. Remove yourself from the fight if you can, but don't let your abuser see you break down.

On the complete opposite side of the abuser's emotional spectrum again, they might completely shut down as soon as you leave a fight or get riled up towards them. They see this as a way of punishing you. And it especially works if you are incredibly attached to your partner.

Withholding communication from someone who thrives on it can really do a number on their confidence, and it can make them feel intensely alone. This isolating feeling is usually enough, after a period of time, to get the victim to forgive the abuser for whatever happened. At that point, the punishment has served its purpose, and the abuser feels dominant once again over the victim. This manipulation tactic is a game of emotional stamina. The victim will never win because the abuser has less of an attachment to the victim than the other way around.

If you're someone on the receiving end of this silent treatment, understand that it's ok for you to feel alone and to want to talk to them again. Try not to let them win. But if you have to give in, just know that you shouldn't have to. Keep your head up and keep a level head.

Rules and restrictions are a massive part of the dynamics between an abuser and the victim of that person's abuse. The abuser controls what the victim can do and when, for how long, and why, so that the victim becomes used to that feeling of being submissive to their partner. However, the rules and restrictions within that relationship aren't always enforced. Intermittent reinforcement is a way for the abuser to keep the victim confused about how to please their partner. Say you did something that the abuser usually likes, and they reward you with praise. You understand the praise and make the connection between the action and the positive result. But what if you do the same thing again a few months later but receive no reward, or your partner even becomes angry with you instead? You expected a positive result, and your partner intentionally upset that expectation by giving you a neutral or negative reaction to the same thing you did.

This negative reaction leaves you wondering what you did wrong and how you can fix it. This gets the victim in the habit of always trying to help and serve their partner. As a victim, don't dwell too much on an unexpected reaction. If need be, just ask them straight out what was different. Make changes if you feel the need to, but only then.

After you've spent a while with your abuser, you might notice a disconnect between the way they treat your issues and reactions versus the way they expect their own to be treated. If you have a problem or you react emotionally to something, your abuser might try to "calm you down" by assuring you that you're simply overreacting. They'll spin your reaction to seem bigger than it was or make it out to be a less proportionate reaction to the actual problem. They might try and assure you that the problem isn't actually a problem, or that you're just making a big deal out of nothing. By comparison, they'll make their own problems and outbursts a top priority, and they expect you to make them your own top priority as well.

This is the abuser's way of making sure you consider their problems before your own. And it also reinforces the idea that the victim should rely more on the abuser's version of what happened than their own, messing up their perception of reality. Again, you should never ever take the way your abuser spins situations as the reality—there is always something they're blowing out of proportion or minimizing to make their own issues look more important. Remember to take care of yourself before anyone else, and always make sure that your health is your own first priority.

The classic abuser will always try to lie to you at every turn. They take every single opportunity they can get to lie to you; cheating you out of your own feelings, making you feel small, and messing up the way you understand reality and the way things actually play out around you. One of the most frequent ways that your abuser might lie to you is through omission.

Lies of omission are not technically lies, but they are a way for your partner to intentionally keep the truth from you or pit you against a friend or family member. This is a way they can keep you away from other people or get you to rely on them and the way they interpret events instead of on your own narrative. If your partner tells you something that happened, you would be inclined to naturally believe them. You might get into a fight with a friend or a loved one and your partner might become your way of interacting with them. Your partner might intentionally keep information from you and prevent you from interacting with that loved one, therefore also preventing you from being able to rely on that loved one and become close with them again. If you can, try to avoid having to rely on your abuser for information and make sure you have a way to fact-check everything they say.

The lies of the abuser culminate in gaslighting, one of the most influential and damaging manipulation tactics that you, as a victim, will experience. Gaslighting occurs when an abuser makes their partner question the way they're interpreting events and wonder if the narrative they're building of the reality around them is actually real. When you and your abuser fight over something, the abuser may try to minimize your reactions and assure you that the way you're getting upset isn't appropriate, because what you're getting upset about didn't actually happen the way you think it did. Insisting that you're incorrect about things you saw or heard, over a long period of time, becomes incredibly damaging to you. You start to question not only your eyes and your perception but your sanity at its core. You start to wonder why you see things the way you do if there's something wrong with you and your own perception. The abuser does this intentionally to get the victim to rely on them more and to get them used to deferring to them.

That deference gives them the power to build whatever narrative they really want. As a victim, observe what parts of the story your abuser always seems to disagree with. Do whatever you can to get a second opinion from someone else and never trust your abuser's story until you can check it with a neutral party who knows what really happened.

When you finally decide to confront your abuser and ask about something, or you even just ask a question that they don't have the kind of answer they need to, they'll evade the question. Abusers spend most of their time evading questions and trying to distract you from what's really going on in the relationship. They'll do anything they can to distract you from reality— they might distract you from the dark parts of their manipulative behavior by trying to suddenly be overly kind to you. Or, on the other hand, they often try to deflect the blame from themselves onto you, instead insinuating that you shouldn't be asking them the question in the first place.

The abuser will often play the victim here, trying to gain your pity by reverting back to the state of someone overcome with trauma and who needs help. They play up this broken act until you finally drop the question and you again shift back to wanting to care for them. They can't allow you to dig too deep or find a weak spot in the narrative they're building. If you're a victim going through this cycle of deflection and evasion, make sure you stay on topic. Don't let yourself be swayed by a rapid change of subject, and don't give in to their emotional manipulation. They can wait until you have your answer to throw a pity party.

Often, abusers will switch back and forth between hot and cold, so to speak. At one point, they may give you the cold shoulder and ignore you at every turn. At some other points in the relationship, they might react violently or aggressively to very small arguments or disagreements over minute things. They do this to keep the victim from being able to settle into a comfortable pattern of thinking. Much like the intermittent reinforcement, the hot and cold back and forth for the abuser is just a way to make sure the victim doesn't get too comfortable associating a certain action with a positive or negative response. If they're constantly being caught off guard by different contradictory reactions, the victim has no secure logic to go off of when it comes to their partner's reactions. Make sure that you have someone else around you who's more stable in your life and who you can rely on. Don't pay any more attention to your abuser's outbursts than you have to.

Similar to their habit of simply leaving out important information, many abusers will also seem to develop a habit of willingly forgetting things that happen that make them look bad. However, they'll very rarely let go of things that have happened that make you look bad.

This is just another way that your abuser will try to put you down and make you believe that you're a bad person or that you don't deserve to be feeling the way that you do. The reason that these tactics work so well is that the victim is probably already relatively used to feeling as though they aren't allowed to feel the way they do, or like they have no right to be upset over something. Someone who has been a victim of abuse in the past might have a hard time letting go of their bad habits and negative ways of thinking from their past abusers.

The current manipulator knows this and takes advantage of the way that many victims already have a tendency to blame themselves. As a victim, know that this is wrong - that this is abuse. Always keep a record to yourself of what happened and when. If you need to, keeping a physical diary of your abuse can help be a comfort when you question if what you experienced was real and valid. Know that toxic relationships very often rely on making you feel crazy and that anything your abuser tries to tell you isn't necessarily true or relevant.

Even if you can confront your abuser and try to get them to understand that something happened exactly the way you thought it did, that doesn't mean that you've suddenly gotten through to that abuser. They'll still find a way to either completely avoid the blame or spin the blame onto you.

This is how the abuser operates—they physically can't take the responsibility for anything, even if it's very obviously their fault. This is the main flaw in the charming and charismatic abuser; they can't own up to anything, even something that is of no detriment to them or something that happened years ago. They're narcissistic, and they find it incredibly difficult to believe that anything that's ever happened was genuinely their fault. They especially won't accept this assertion from someone they look down on and regularly abuse.

This deflection of blame is actually usually more about their own flaws than it is about cornering and blaming their victim instead. But this blame is usually a byproduct of their inability to take the blame for anything. As a victim, put yourself first and distance yourself from the abuser if you feel the need to. Your safety and health are both more important than the comfort of your abuser, and you need to be able to properly prioritize yourself. Understand that your abuser acting out and generally being childish is not your fault—no way that they treat you is ever your fault.

Hypnosis might not be something you think of when you consider the way that you might be a victim of abuse. But trance can play a fairly large role when it comes to how your abuser affects you and what they do to you, how they alter the way you think and to what extent. We all go into some state of trance at some point in our lives, whether it be when we're driving down the road or really intensely focused on our favorite book.

Trance is a heightened state of focus, but it's also a state in which we have a lack of focus on the things going on around us. Abusers have a similar effect on their victims sometimes, make it so that the victim can't help but only focus on their relationship with the abuser while their other relationships fade out of that focus. That lets the abuser truly cut the victim off from the outside world and take advantage of them to the fullest extent.

Don't let the abuser give you this sense of tunnel vision! If you let yourself only focus on the abuser, you let them win. Make sure you keep in touch with people outside the relationship and do your best to keep those relationships alive and well. You may need to rely on them in the future, so make sure your focus isn't completely limited to the abuser. The person right in front of you isn't ever the only one that matters.

When the abuser fights you about the way things happen, it won't always be in a way that makes it obvious that they're actually trying to fight you. They're trying to win the argument, and they're also trying to break you down and make you question your sanity. To do this, they'll phrase their denial in a patronizing, passive-aggressive way. Their goal at this point is just to make sure you aren't sure of yourself or your perception. You may be fighting over something with them, and they'll refute your claims in a more passive way. Where they might have otherwise simply told you that you were wrong before presenting their "side" of the story, they'll now accuse you of other things. Instead of saying "no, it happened this way," they'll begin to ask, "are you sure that's what happened?" They ask this way to make it seem like they're trying to help you or give you the benefit of the doubt so that they don't seem too combative.

In reality, they know you're already questioning yourself a lot, and they intend to capitalize on that uncertainty. Make sure you can keep an actual documentation of what actually happened. Or at least have someone you can talk to who has a neutral understanding of the events and can process them in an unbiased way. The abuser just wants to upset you before pulling you back in and making it seem like they're a good person.

This façade, this trick that spells out that they're actually a good—or at least a broken and helpless person, is the most dangerous one you'll encounter during your time with the abuser. They'll push you away and abuse and drive you insane but draw you right back in as soon as you start to pull away on your own. They know what you want out of them and they're more than willing to dangle it right in front of you until they know they can do whatever they want with you. They know exactly how to appeal to your desire to help them, your desire to help anyone you meet who's gone through something similar to you.

In the infinite cruelty of the manipulative abuser, they understand your despair and the things you've been through and they know how much you want to help them. Although they don't want the pity of your real help, they do want to keep you in their life so they can keep preying on you. This is what you really have to realize while in an abusive relationship. Your abuser does not care about you, does not care about your feelings, and does not want your help. This is hurtful to finally realize but understanding it and taking control of that fact will help you get out of a terrible relationship. Even though your abuser doesn't want your help, you can still help yourself.

Chapter 10. Tactics to Break Free From Psychological and Emotional Abuse

Making the decision to break free is difficult. Every single relationship that has ever ended would have been hard at the end. Nobody wants to walk away from someone they have many memories with, and it might be that you even still love this person, but you know that they're not right for you. That is perhaps the hardest situation of them all.

When you love someone, even if the feeling isn't reciprocated, you desperately don't want to leave. You start thinking about how life is going to be without them, and you wonder how you're going to enjoy a day without their presence. All of this is normal, but it's important to remember that time is a great healer. You should also focus on the reality of the situation - when you walk away and you begin to heal, you will no longer have to deal with those manipulation tactics that cause you to doubt your own sanity and cause health issues. You will be free, and able to live your life away from negative tactics and manipulation.

Of course, it's very easy to say, but very hard to do. Everything is easy when you're not the one in the situation, but the fact remains that you're not the first, and unfortunately, you won't be the last. There are countless men and women who are stuck in manipulative relationships. Some know they're in a toxic relationship, some have an inkling but don't want to face up to it, and some have no idea.

The longer you stay in a relationship which is slowly draining the life out of you, the more damage will be done. The slow drip of gaslighting builds into a flood, and by the end, you will literally be a shell of your former self. You will have no discernment about what is right or wrong, and you will doubt every single person around you, apart from your partner. In the end, that is what they want - they want you to be dependent on them. And a malignant narcissist will want you dependent on them for your every thought.

You have to come to the firm realization of what is going on, in order to be able to be just as firm in your conviction to leave. Do bear in mind however that every single relationship is different and that means every single means of escape will be equally unique. You may leave and not hear from your partner for weeks on end, or you might be bombarded from the second they realize you're gone. You have no way of predicting what is going to happen, and the only thing you can do is set the groundwork in place to ensure that you can exit the relationship in the easiest way possible, without more trauma than you've already been subjected to.

This chapter is going to outline five specific tactics to help you break free from psychological and emotional abuse. We can't stress enough at this point the need for a support network. You should not have to do this alone. The fact is that you will not be as successful if you do it alone than if you have at least one person around you. This person can be your rock when things are tough and can be there to help you overcome the emotions that are bound to take over as you heal from the scars of what has happened to you.

What you need to understand very clearly is that by attempting to leave this relationship, you are doing something extremely brave and strong. You are not running away, you are not a failure and you're not weak. Your partner may tell you these things, but they are wrong. You are putting yourself first and that is something you need to do from this point on. If your partner tries to show you their charming side, their vulnerable side, you need to sidestep it. This is not something genuine, this is a mask and an act which should not be trusted.

Technique 1

Keep a Journal and Write Everything Down

When you write something down, you're committing it to memory. There is a reason that busy people carry a notebook in their bag or pocket, or perhaps use a notebook app on their phone. This is because when you write something down, it's there to read back, and you're not going to forget. In addition, other details aren't going to blur what you're trying to remember or perhaps distort it out of proportion.

It's best to write things down manually, rather than use an app. The reason is that the manual act of writing helps to solidify details in your mind. When you type, there is no real association with the words and your brain, it's just literally characters on a screen. However, when you use a pen and paper, you're forming the letters and sounding out the words in your mind as you write them. This helps to commit details to memory.

What should you journal? Anything that you feel you need to. This can be a diary-style journal, i.e. what happened that day, how you felt, what was said, what your partner said or did; or it can be a bullet-point style list of things that you feel are important. It's a good idea to keep this journal with you and scribble things down as you go, or you can sit at the end of the day and debrief yourself. However, if you do this at the end of the day and there is an altercation between you and your partner before you have a chance to journal, some of the details you wanted to write down could become twisted or unclear. Writing things as you go, therefore, helps with accuracy and clarity.

This journal, if kept over a month or possibly even more, will make for very interesting reading when you look back over it. It's vital that when you choose to read it back, you're in an even state of mind. Don't read it back when you're feeling emotional, or after a fight or upset with your partner. Do it when you're calm, relaxed and on an even keel. This will allow you to see the reality of what is going on.

The information contained within this journal should pave your road to freedom, but it also acts as a way of confirming the truth in your mind. When someone tries to manipulate you, they do so in order to change your perception of an event, as I've mentioned several times before. With no point of reference, you start to question whether you're making things up, seeing things that didn't really happen, or you're twisting small details and making them more important than they really are. When you have it written down in front of you - there in black and white - you know what happened. You have proof - a point to reinforce what you knew all along.

The more you see things in black and white, and then hear your partner try and twist it into something different, the more confident you will feel in yourself and your own perception and clarity. This will be a tool to help open your eyes to the manipulation that is going on, and remove doubts about whether leaving is the right option or not.

When something is written in front of you, written at the time of it happening, it's impossible to ignore. When something happens once, you can put it down to "one of those things", but when it happens multiple times, it's a certain sign of something harmful going on. Having a journal with details written down gives you something to read back over when you're feeling unsure and something which will prove to be a vital confirmation tool.

Your journal will also help you stay away from your partner after you leave them. When a relationship ends, it's easy to start thinking about the good times, and it fills you with regrets. This can be enough to force you to go back if you're not feeling strong enough or if you don't have a good enough support network around you. Your journal will form part of your support network too. When you have these "wobbles", you can read back over your journal and remember why you left.

In many ways, your journal may become your rational brain when your emotions and your memories start to take over.

Technique 2

Identify Your Support Buddy and Tell Them as Much as You Can

Your journal is not going to help you by itself - you need a support network around you. Identify one person who you want to nominate as your support buddy, but of course, make sure that they're happy to be the nominated person!

Without a doubt, anyone who is your friend or family member is going to jump at the chance to help you out of this situation. In fact, they've probably been waiting for this opportunity for a long time. They want you to be free, they want to see you happy again and be back to your normal self.

In order to help them understand exactly what's going on, you need to bravely sit down and tell them as much as you can. Of course, if you don't want to share specific, private details, you don't have to, but simply let them know the severity of how things have deteriorated, how you feel, and that you want to leave. Explain that you know that your partner is not going to let you go that easily and that you may question your actions. Tell them that you want them to help you stay on track, and not to go back and that you need someone you can rely on if you start to have doubts or worries.

This person doesn't need to be with you 24/7, of course, they have their own life too, but everyone is able to pick up a telephone. But do consider that you might need to go and stay with a friend or family member in the immediate aftermath of leaving your partner, if you live with them currently or if you have your own place but you know they're going to knock on your door. You can ask to stay at your nominated support buddy's house or you can go somewhere else, just make sure that your support buddy knows where that is.

Many people struggle with asking for help. There's no reason why this should be the case, because when you care about someone you're happy to help them no matter what. Again, you're not weak for asking for help, you're strong. This is the bravest thing you will ever do and if you have to write that down and repeat it as a po sitive affirmation or mantra, then do so.

Just remember that you cannot and should not do this alone.

Technique 3

If You Aren't at the Point of Leaving, Set Boundaries Which Should Not be Crossed

Maybe you're not ready to leave yet. In that case, what do you do? Are you a little unsure that the relationship isn't quite on the manipulative end of the scale, but it's potentially about to tip over? Again, nobody should ever deal with abusive behavior, but it is your choice whether you leave or not. We have to point that out everyone has free will.

If however you think you are in a relationship with a narcissist, but it's not severe, and you feel like you want to try one last thing, something you can do is set boundaries.

Will this work? It really depends on your partner and the type of relationship you have. In any case, setting boundaries can be a way to build up the courage to leave, but you must stick to these boundaries and do exactly as you say.

For example, let's say that your partner is sometimes verbally abusive. This doesn't happen all the time, but sometimes they become angry and say things, which they then say they didn't mean. Firstly, you do not deserve to be verbally abused and you should seriously consider your future in this relationship. However, if you do want to attempt to right this problem, you need to set a boundary.

You would do this by sitting down with your partner and firmly explaining that you do not like it when they are verbally abusive. Be specific and point out the types of things they say, for instance, "I don't like it when you call me names", or "I don't like it when you shout at me". This helps your partner to understand the specific type of behavior you're referring to and helps to set your boundary in stone.

You would then explain your boundary. This could be that the next time they call you names you're going to walk out and not return until they apologize. This is just an example. Then, you need to really stick to your guns. If it does happen again, you need to do as you have said; you need to walk out and wait for the apology.

A very final boundary could be "the next time you shout at me, I am going to leave you", and mean it. That is your final call and one which will need you to do exactly what you say, so don't make this a boundary if you're not ready to actually go through with it.

If you say you're going to do something and then don't actually do it, you're crying wolf. Your partner is not going to take your words seriously and they will simply continue doing what you've told them you don't like. This will mean the abusive behavior continues in a loop and causes further discomfort and upset.

Another useful boundary is refusing to listen. Again, you need to sit down and tell your partner exactly what you're going to do. If you don't do this, your actions may get lost in the moment and have no meaning. The walking away or not listening boundary involves you getting up and silently walking out of the room or out of the house whenever your partner shows the behavior that you do not like. You have to tell your partner the specific behavior your action is going to be linked to, and you need to explain what you will do. This should act as a deterrent, but if it does happen (and quite frankly, it probably will), you need to avoid reacting. Do not show emotion, simply stand up and walk away.

Narcissists, in particular, have to have their specific needs met. They want a reaction and you're not giving it to them. Yes, it will drive them crazy and could exacerbate their behavior, but why should you sit there and listen to it? Walking away shows that you have the power to recognize the action as abusive, and take yourself out of the situation. The more you do this, the stronger you will feel.

Of course, it's far better for you in the long-term to simply walk away from a relationship that causes you these specific problems in your life. There is a happier future waiting for you, and prolonging the pain and upset is simply wasting your own time and tears. Despite that, it could be that you need to gain strength before walking away, and setting boundaries will allow you to do that.

Technique 4

Focus on Yourself and Allow Your Confidence to Grow

When you finally realize that you are the victim of manipulation and abuse, it's very easy to feel like you've failed. You have not failed. At this time, your confidence is probably at an all-time low, so you need to build up your confidence to find the strength to walk away. Setting boundaries does that to a certain degree, but focusing on yourself is a great way to give you insight into what your life is going to be like post-relationship, and how much happier and healthier you will be for it.

It's far easier to make decisions clearly when you feel good about yourself. When you're battered down by manipulation, making choices can be extremely hard. If you've been subjected to gaslighting, you're going to question most choices and that means the decision to leave is going to be extremely hard.

A good way to build up that confidence is to shift the spotlight of attention away from your partner and focus it on yourself alone. Don't tell your partner what you're going to do, simply do it. If you remember our signs of manipulation, one very successful tactic that narcissists use is to downplay any interests or hobbies you have. They see these activities as a threat and they don't want you engaging in them, because of the confidence they give you and the opportunities to meet other people. If you tell your partner that you're going to start going to the gym, you're going to start an evening class, or you're going to go jogging after work, they're going to do everything they can to dissuade you.

For that reason, simply do it and don't tell them.

Focusing on yourself can be anything you want it to be. It can be changing your diet and eating healthier, joining the gym and getting some exercise, joining a team sport and enjoying training and matches on a regular basis, reconnecting with old friends that you might have been spending less time with, learning a new skill - it could even be going away for the weekend on your own, simply because you want to! Start making decisions solely for your own enjoyment and to build up your confidence. At the moment, you likely do everything for your partner and you don't think about your own needs. That has to change.

In order to be healthier in your mind, you need to be healthier in your own body too. Look at your diet. Look at how much exercise you get. Cut down on drinking and smoking, and drink more water. Do everything to make yourself feel better, but focus on wellness and healthy choices.

The confidence you will feel will be enough to lift you up and, when used in conjunction with other techniques such as journaling, you will find the inner strength to make the ultimate choice for your own future - to leave and break free for good.

Technique 5

Make a Firm Plan

Now it's time to make a plan. If you have no ties, leaving could be quite easy, logistically speaking. For instance, if you don't live together, you likely don't share finances, you don't have any mutual friends, and you likely don't have children. However, the likelihood is that you do have some kind of shared interests.

If you do live together, or are married, the situation can be a little more complicated and you need to make a plan in terms of what you're going to do in order to make life after the split easier on you.

Ask yourself the following questions:

• Where are you going to live? Will you stay in a place that the gaslighter knows about?

• Do you need to go and stay with someone else for a short period of time after you walk away?

• Do you have enough money to live independently?

- Do you have children together? If so, how are you going to orchestrate the break up and how are you going to ensure they get to see their other parent (if that is appropriate)?

- If you are married, how easy is it going to be to get a divorce?

- Do you have shared assets?

While it's hard to think this clearly when you're in the middle of deciding to leave someone you love, it's important to know what you're going to do and how you're going to do it. Building your confidence and sharing the load with a trusted support buddy is going to help you out here, and the process of actually planning will make you more certain that you're doing the right thing. That way, there will be no going back, and you'll know it has to be that way.

Sit down and work things out. If you need to get professional help from a lawyer beforehand, that's perfectly fine. Knowing your rights and the best way to split assets without extra contact is useful. It's also certainly worthwhile getting help and advice in terms of what happens if you have children. Is there a reason that your children shouldn't see their other parent? But, always remember that your children have a right to see both of their parents, unless there is a serious reason which would prevent them from doing so, for their own safety and welfare.

Seek professional advice on all of these matters without commitment, in a totally impartial manner, and you will be able to walk away with a clearer mind. This will also minimize and limit the amount of time you need to be in contact with your then ex-partner, or you could nominate a legal representative to do the dealings for you if that is something you feel more comfortable with.

These five specific techniques will help you to break free from a manipulative relationship.

Technicalities can sometimes be enough to cause someone to stay in a relationship, simply because they don't know what to do to get out of it, or how they're going to survive outside of it financially. By arming yourself with the correct knowledge, you can ensure that you break free in the best possible way.

The main points to bear in mind from this chapter are:

• Breaking free from a manipulative relationship isn't easy, but preparing yourself will make the waters a little calmer.

• Journaling can be a very useful way to help solidify details in your mind and give you the confidence and clarity you need to make the break.

• A support network is vital, but you should nominate one specific person to be your in-depth buddy. You don't have to tell this person everything, but you should tell them as much as you feel comfortable, so they can see things through your eyes as much as possible.

• Setting boundaries can be a way to prepare yourself to walk away and build confidence. It can also be a way of attempting to right a situation one last time, before walking away.

• If you're wondering whether to go the route of setting boundaries as a last resort, always remember that nobody deserves to be manipulated or abused. So ask yourself whether this relationship is worth trying to save.

• Focusing on your own health, wellbeing, and confidence will allow you to feel stronger and able to make the break more successfully.

• It's important to make a plan for everything you need after the break. This includes housing, finances, shared assets, and any issues with regards to children or divorce.

• Seek impartial legal advice on any issues you're not sure of, before the break.

• You should avoid all contact with your ex-partner after the break, but it may be that you need to discuss certain things, such as children, divorce proceedings, or how to split shared assets. You can nominate a legal representative to do those things for you if you really do not feel you can meet and discuss face to face with your ex-partner.

Chapter 11. Healing from Gaslighting

A narcissist will try to influence your friends, family and coworkers to turn against you and isolate you. His charm and persuasiveness turns your circle of influence into his own little 'hive' – people who now buzz around him and believe everything he says about you. This is the worst damage he can do, and, while you can successfully escape the abuse, this damage can take months, years or even decades to recover from.

The victim will feel rattled after having gone through something akin to what a prisoner of war has suffered at the hands of the narcissist and his hive. The hive, which has never experienced these things, will not understand or believe what the victim is talking about. They will think that the victim's experiences are 'made up', 'fake', 'imagined'.

The abuse victim is again thrust into abuse at the hands of others who do not seek to understand his or her experience. He or she is not afforded even simple understanding and validation for the experiences that they have gone through.

The victim is confused about whether or not he is the victim or the perpetrator of the abuse, having been blame-shifted by the narcissist and the hive. The narcissist and the hive flips into victim mode themselves to mirror what it is that the victim is projecting.

There is power in numbers, and the hive knows that yelling more loudly than the victim will make the hive and the narcissist seem like the victim instead. Everyone comes to the aid of the wounded narcissist and his hive.

People naturally want to side with those who are popular, and it is easy to see that no one is taking the side of the narcissist's victim. This makes the decision to side with the victim an unpopular decision, and no one wants to be on the unpopular side. The victim will be reeling once he or she realizes that the narcissist has even stolen support from his or her own inner circle, which is a final nail in their coffin.

Most victims of gaslighting and narcissistic overt and covert abuse retreat to lick their wounds. They are devastated to see that opinions and ideas are so fluid and so shifting in the wake of the narcissist.

Their own perception is the truth of what really happened; however, no one else subscribes to their version of reality.

Even worse, other people will seek to convince true victims that their reality is false, contrary to their own experience and their own eyes.

This leaves the victims of gaslighting largely alone to heal their own wounds. The must rebuild their own lives and their own future.

Victims must reclaim their lost identity in the wake of the narcissistic abuse and the attack from the hive.

Victims must reach back into their childhood to reassemble the broken pieces of who they once were, and to seek to define a new identity that can be reborn from the ashes of the devastation left by the narcissist and the hive.

Victims must move forward to build a new arsenal of memories from newly created experiences, adventures and memories in their lives. They must live with intention. They must live with purpose.

Abuse victims must find new purpose after the devastation that comes from the hive and from the narcissist. They must discover and work on their own goals, as well as supporting others in a positive way.

Most survivors of narcissistic abuse go on to tell their stories. They go on to warn others of abuse. They go on to protect and advocate for the victims of domestic violence and narcissistic abuse. They go on to educate others about the abuse that they have experienced from the hive and from the narcissist. They go on to define the things that they have felt, thought, heard. They go on to warn others that the hive is coming for them, and to help them build a wall to protect themselves against the hive.

The survivors must band together to fight narcissistic abuse and gaslighting. They must be there for each other, to support and encourage one another.

Survivors must form their own hive and a protective barrier together against the hives of the narcissist. These new hives must have ethics and morals and loving inclusion – however, they must not have an open door to the narcissists and the hives that power their disorder.

The Future for a Narcissist and You

What does the future hold? Nobody has a crystal ball, but the bottom line is this - if you are in a manipulative relationship, the only realistic option you have is to get out of it and work towards righting the damage that has been done. The future will continue as the present is now, and chances are the manipulation and its damaging effects will become worse still. Manipulation and psychological abuse do not just simply stop; they continue onwards and the effects snowball to the point of no return.

There is no future for a relationship of this kind. As sad as it is, and as much as you may not want to hear it, that is the truth.

Breaking up is Hard to do But Always The Right Thing

A "regular" relationship, i.e. a relationship which isn't affected by narcissism and manipulation is difficult to end. If you're the person doing the ending you might agonize over your decision for months, you might question if you're doing the right thing and tie yourself up in knots. When you finally end the relationship, you might regret it for a while, wonder if you did the right thing and second guess your actions.

This is normal.

So, when a narcissistic or manipulative relationship is forced to end, you're going to feel the same emotions, but with even more confusion thrown in for good measure.

Breaking up is always hard, whether you're the one doing the breaking up or you're the one being broken up with. There is no easy way to end a union with a person who you have shared a lot of time, memories, and feelings with. If you could walk away from such a relationship with ease, you would be heartless and lacking in empathy yourself, possibly making you a borderline narcissist!

For that reason, don't misunderstand the feeling of grief when the relationship ends with making a mistake. Breaking up is hard, but in this situation, it is always the right thing to do. There is no way you can continue in a relationship which causes you upset, psychological and emotional damage and causes you to constantly doubt yourself and your own sanity. That isn't healthy, and that isn't loving.

It's easy to say you deserve better, but everyone does. Nobody deserves to be manipulated and abused in this way. This is the cruelest way to treat a person: to cause them to become a shell of their former selves, to take a vibrant, full-of-life person and turn them into someone so lacking in confidence and self-assuredness, they don't know which way is up or down. That isn't someone who loves you, that's someone who wants to control you and manipulate you.

It's also very difficult to get your head around the fact that someone, a human being, would cause this much pain to another person. That is sometimes one of the reasons why people stay in these types of relationships because they can't quite fathom why someone they thought so highly of could act in such a cruel way. The problem is that the person they thought they knew isn't the real person underneath the mask.

A narcissist doesn't have the same feelings as a regular person, they don't have empathy and that means they don't feel guilt or remorse when they hurt another person. A normal person would feel guilty or bad if they saw someone they cared about cry, but a narcissist doesn't have this in them or, if they have an inkling of it, it's not enough to stop them behaving the way they do.

A narcissist is never going to develop empathy without very intensive therapy, and that's something a true narcissist is not going to do. Without the acknowledgment of a problem, treatment won't work, and narcissists do not believe there is anything wrong with them.

So, what options do you have?

You can carry on in the relationship and hope things improve. Obviously, the chances of that occurring are extremely slim. The other option is that you can leave the relationship and work towards a brighter future.

For your own sake, we hope you choose the latter.

Why a Narcissist Will Never be Happy

A narcissist, a true narcissist, has a personality disorder and unless they seek treatment, they will never be free of the constraints which the condition imposes upon them.

When you look at narcissism from the outside, without actually knowing anyone with the condition or having been a victim of someone who manipulated and abused, it might be easy to feel sorry for narcissists. They do not have empathy and therefore cannot love in the same way. They don't feel things the same as others and can't connect with others in the same way.

Due to the complex effects of this type of personality disorder, narcissists will never be able to be truly happy. Their constant need to gain control over other people, and their constant self-centered way of thinking, are what make this type of personalities lone wolves.

The future for a narcissist is much the same as it is now. Empty. Cognitive behavioral therapy and deep mindset training are the only ways to overcome narcissism, but this first requires acknowledgment of the problem and a willingness to work hard to overcome it. A narcissist is highly unlikely to ever admit they are wrong, so they're not going to admit that they need help because of their entire personality traits either.

This means that most narcissists will continue in the same way for the rest of their lives. Friendships will fall by the wayside, relationships will start and end, and people will talk about how they were manipulated and hurt by them. It's sad to think that help is out there but rarely taken advantage of; but again, you can't force someone to face a problem if they refuse to admit it's there in front of them.

This truth, however, should not stop you from walking away. Yes, it's sad that a narcissist will never truly be happy, but you need to focus on your happiness. Your happiness does not lie in the hands of a narcissist or any type of manipulative person. It lies in your hands alone.

Your Future Will Become Brighter Over Time

At this point, you might be feeling confused, emotional, unsure, and worried. Take heart that those emotions are entirely normal for a person in your situation.

What you need to hold onto is the fact that your future will become much brighter over time. It's almost like someone has a remote control in their hand and at the moment, the brightness setting is on very low, almost to the point where you can't see what's on the screen. The brightness will remain low until after the break is made, and at some point immediately afterward, the brightness might dim ever so slightly further, but only for a second. After that, it's as though someone is slowly turning up the brightness a notch every day until you finally reach a point where the brightness is almost blinding.

You will get there, but you have to give it time. You cannot rush the healing process, and you need to allow it to follow through in the right way. You have lost someone you love, and you need to fully grieve that. But you also need to unravel the manipulation you've been subjected to and straighten out your mind once more.

All of this takes time, but it's time well spent.

Your future does not have to be the same as it is now, it can be brighter, and it will be brighter if you take the brave step to break free from the clutches of manipulation, putting the brightness control back in your own hands.

Having to walk away from someone you care about is tough, but it's necessary if you want to live a happier life in the future. You deserve that happier life.

The main points to take away from this chapter are:

• In order to be happy you need to extract yourself from a psychologically and emotionally manipulative relationship.

• If you stay in the relationship, your situation will remain the same or may even worsen.

• A narcissist will never be happy because people will continually leave them, due to the abuse they subject people to.

• Narcissists are unlikely to change because they will never admit there is a problem and get treatment.

• Your future will be brighter if you make the break, but you need to allow the grieving and healing process to happen, which all takes time.

You deserve better!

Conclusion

If you are a victim of gaslighting or suspect that someone might be gaslighting you, then reading this book is a good first step toward protecting yourself from the effects of gaslighting and recovery. But reading alone is not enough. Practicing what you read can be the difference between staying stuck in the shadow of a gaslighter and being the independent individual that you are meant to be.

It is not only children in the formative ages who can be influenced by their environment. Even as adults, the people we spend time with can affect us positively or negatively. Living, working and associating with someone who constantly reminds you of how incompetent, weak, and unfit you are is not healthy for your emotional health. Surrounding yourself with positivity is not merely a New Age gibberish. The implication of doing the opposite can be quite devastating. Unfortunately, even if you inadvertently stick with negative people, it will still wreak its havoc.

For this reason, if you discover that someone is gaslighting you, your best option is to discontinue your relationship with them. You may be in a position where you cannot cut off all ties immediately, but you should work toward that end.

Don't let past good experiences blind you from the unpleasant experiences an abusive person is presently putting you through. You need to move past sentimentality and be more rational to regain your freedom and rebuild your life again.

If you have suffered emotional abuse, especially gaslighting, you may conclude that you are frail, pathetic, and won't be able to take on the challenge of doing without the gaslighter in your life. Don't believe that lie. It is the gaslighter's spiteful narrative that is trying to trick you into losing faith in yourself. You are not frail or pathetic. Instead, you are strong because it takes a strong individual to survive gaslighting abuse. Don't let anyone tell you otherwise!

And no, you are not paranoid or too sensitive if you think that your colleague or business partner is undermining you. You are also not mistrusting if you have reason to believe that your spouse or romantic partner is being unfaithful. If you have a hunch, follow it without making accusations. The gaslighter may have tricked your conscious mind, but they can't squelch your unconscious mind. This is why even though you may buy into their lies you still feel an inner discordance with your truth. Trust your gut. Many mysteries have unfolded and cases been solved based on nothing but a hunch. You may not be right all the time, but the more you listen to your intuition, the stronger it gets and the more you trust yourself.

Ridding yourself of a gaslighter creates a vacuum in your life that needs to be filled. I am not suggesting that you should jump from an abusive relationship into the next available relationship. However, as you eliminate the bad influence from your life, it is wise to replace it with something empowering. Never neglect the need to stay in constant touch with a support system that will help to boost your sense of self. Get connected to support groups, trusted friends, and dependable family members who you can draw inspiration from. Leaving an abusive person without finding a positive substitute does little to speed up your recovery and leaves you vulnerable. Your journey to recovery is only secured with the help of positive reinforcements.

Remember that the bulk of your work is internal and intangible but carries a lot of impact. Ending your relationship or friendship is necessary in most cases, but it is physical and external. Blocking an abuser's phone number, deleting their contact details, and severing all forms of communication is necessary, but these things are all physical and external. You can still undo them. But recognizing your true self-worth, building your self-esteem, learning to love and trust yourself more are intangible, internal, and have more influence on your behavior. You can physically end a relationship but still want to be with that person despite their causing you so much pain. But if you learn to recognize your worth, you will not want to be with someone who treats you with disdain.

What are you waiting for? Go ahead and start implementing the strategies and tips in this book. Set new goals and set your mind to achieve them. Stick with them and follow through, and you will soon be the confident and happy person you deserve to be!

Printed in Great Britain
by Amazon

33736790R00059